ELITE SALES SPECIALISTS

26 INSPIRATIONAL **SALES** & **BUSINESS** STORIES FROM **TOP INDUSTRY LEADERS**

NICK STAAB & GRADUATES

Publisher: Addea Media
Year of Publication: 2024
ISBN: 978-1-7399431-5-8

I would like to dedicate this book to my family:
My mum and dad, Kathy, and Paul;
My two brothers, Mark, and Darren;
My four nephews, Daniel, Tom, Josh, and Charlie.
To my loving Fiancée Suz Hawkins (Soon To be Suz Staab)
And lastly to my amazing mentees of the Elite Sales Academy.
Loving sales, loving serving, loving life!

Nick Staab

CONTENTS

ACKNOWLEDGEMENTS

I am eternally grateful to Dea Fileva, who helped me write and edit this book after helping me launch my first book 'Selling Is Serving' to the top of the charts in 2022.

To all of my clients in the Elite Sales Academy for being such amazing action takers, especially the 25 of you who have taken your time to share your powerful, transformational stories in this book.

To my loving parents Paul and Kathy and amazing family who made me the man I am today.

To my amazing business partner Liam Ryan.

To my number one fan Suz Hawkins (soon to be Suz Staab).

And to all of my readers, for their interest, precious time and comments.

Thank you.

This book has been written by contributors from around the world, and to preserve the authenticity of their voices we have retained their preferred spelling, grammar, and punctuation conventions.

BEFORE WE DIVE IN

To explain why I wrote this book with graduates of my training business *The Elite Sales Academy*, it all really comes down to three simple words.

'Selling Is Serving'.

I believe that if you're not open to somebody trying to sell to you, you're closed to somebody trying to help you.

That is why 'Selling Is Serving' is the main ethos of The Elite Sales Academy. It's the heartbeat that we all share when it comes to selling our products and services to others. If you have a product or a service that will solve other people's problems, you must do whatever it takes to ethically sell that person your solution via the skills of influence and persuasion.

I want to inspire as many people as I can to step up and start serving others.

Existing business owners, people in jobs working for others, retired, students, you name it, I have helped people of all backgrounds grow a successful business via the main key principle of selling and serving others.

When I wrote my first best-selling book, Selling Is Serving, in 2022, it flew to the top of the charts on release. It reached the number one best-selling book in 21 different categories and made it into Amazon's top 100 books of all categories of fiction and non-fiction releases.

This book allowed me to catapult my training business The Elite Sales Academy to be one of the UK's fastest-growing sales businesses which did amazing things for me, however, there were still a number of people who would make statements along this line of 'Well, it's alright for you growing a business Nick, you were born good at sales'.

Now my typical response to these claims are normally something like 'No, I was born a baby just like you. I just invested into the best trainers I could access and worked as hard as I could'.

As my mission is to inspire as many people as I can to love sales, I felt it would be an amazing opportunity for my next book to not only include my inspirational story and top tips for business, but the inspirational stories and top tips of other people from all walks of life and business.

This book is not only written by me but also by 25 of my successful case studies from all different businesses and backgrounds, whom I refer to as 'Elite Sales Specialists' (hence the book name).

Sit back and become empowered by the 26 stories of Elite Sales Specialists coming up in this book and implement the top three tips that they have discovered in their businesses, to get the upper hand in your own and become head and shoulders above everybody else.

For those action-takers who make it to the end of the book, you will be rewarded with a special gift upon completion. Also, if you have any questions or comments, you can find The Elite Sales

Academy contact details at the end of the book in the 'Become An Elite Sales Specialist' Section.

Enjoy.

Nick Staab
Best Selling Author & Founder of The Elite Sales Academy

CHAPTER 1

Selling Is Serving: The Journey from Cold to Sold

NICK STAAB

'Selling Is Serving, it is an act of service. I firmly believe that mastering the art of sales is a paramount skill that everyone should acquire to ensure financial certainty and to lead a life brimming with abundance.'

- Nick Staab

I AM PASSIONATE ABOUT instilling confidence and conviction in individuals when it comes to selling and empowering them to embrace the sales process with enthusiasm. My life's mission is dedicated to serving and guiding as many people as possible to master the art of ethical selling. My motivation stems from the belief that sales is an indispensable skill, both in the realm of business and everyday life. Unfortunately, it's a concept often shrouded in fear and misconception, deemed a 'dirty word' by many. My unwavering mission is to challenge and transform this perception, making sales an accessible and honourable practice for all.

My journey into sales began on the opposite side of the globe from my home in Essex, England, at the tender age of 22. I found myself in Sydney, Australia, having recently completed my master's degree in IT and Computing. Faced with the common post-graduation job hunt struggles, I opted for a gap year to explore the world and discover my purpose before I settled down on a career path.

I was that determined yet naive kid who went door to door, aiming to convince Australian residents to switch their energy providers and reduce their bills. It didn't take long for me to realise that to avoid doors being slammed in my face, I needed to invest in mastering the art of selling. But what truly amazed me was the limitless earning potential through uncapped commissions. Each customer I successfully closed meant AUD $50 in my pocket. If I could achieve this with five customers a day, it translated to AUD $250 daily, AUD $1,250 weekly, and an impressive AUD $4,000 per month. This was the moment I saw what some people never see, and that was the true potential of ceilingless earnings that rewarded me for my ability and performance.

It was a straightforward equation: improve my selling skills, and my performance would improve, resulting in higher earnings. The correlation was undeniable.

I delved deep into the vast resources available on the internet, devoured books, and tirelessly absorbed knowledge on the subjects of selling and negotiation. In no time, I not only met but exceeded my income goals while I was just a 22-year-old backpacker. This achievement left me earning more than some of my own family members, who were advising me to follow the traditional employment path.

When my visa expired, I returned home, fuelled by a newfound passion for excelling in sales while doing what I loved. I secured a position at a prominent health and fitness chain where I could earn a commission, and I steadily ascended the corporate hierarchy.

A pivotal moment in my journey occurred on Monday, 18th June 2018, during a meeting with my regional manager, Jay. To describe Jay, he stood at a mere 5 feet, his bald head gleamed under the light, and he perched his glasses at the tip of his nose. He had an intense gaze that seemed to penetrate your soul and a penchant for wielding his authority in a rather overbearing manner. Nothing I or anyone else did ever seemed to meet his exacting standards. Have you ever encountered someone like that?

During our meeting, Jay's words seemed to pass right through me, as my mind was elsewhere. Earlier that morning, during my two-hour commute into London, I had received a text message from my mom. It contained the dates for my Nan's funeral, who fell fate to a painful loss from cancer that had occurred just two weeks prior.

As the meeting came to a close, Jay stood up and banged his papers on the desk. I took a big gulp of oxygen and summoned the courage to say, 'Jay, you know my Nan passed away? I just received the dates for the funeral. It's going to be on Thursday, June 28th.'

Jay replied remorselessly, 'Ah, sorry, Nick. No time off at the end of the month. It's not me; it's company policy.'

'You know what, Jay, screw you and your job!'

... is what I wanted to say.

However, I found myself unable to voice those words. It had taken me five long years to ascend the slippery rungs of the corporate ladder, only to discover that I had been diligently climbing the wrong rooftop all along.

It was as if a crushing weight had descended upon me, and at that moment, the stark realisation hit me: I was nothing more than a faceless cog within a corporate machine. I had poured my heart and soul into this company, consistently arriving early, leaving late, taking on extra shifts, enduring a gruelling two-hour commute into London, and repeating the journey six to seven times a week. When I finally returned home, I was not the best version of myself; exhaustion and irritability had become my constant companions, perhaps contributing to the demise of my previous relationship.

Echoing the wisdom of Albert Einstein, who famously remarked that 'the definition of insanity is doing the same thing over and over again', I recognised the pressing need for a change in my life. However, I faced a dilemma—I couldn't allow my mounting frustration to seep into my work, as it would undoubtedly affect my ability to serve my clients and, in turn, impact my earnings. A week passed, and I did attend the funeral, but I couldn't shake off the feeling that something profound had withered away within me.

A month later, a pivotal moment occurred. I was on the train home one evening from Paddington to Liverpool Street, and someone on the train was trying to reach their hand out to me and help me. In fact, they had been trying to do this for many weeks now, and I kept pushing him away. 'Leave me alone, go away, I'm not interested!'

I was sitting on the train scrolling through Facebook, and a guy popped up on my screen. He had a big set of white teeth, and he was saying, 'How to turn your passions into profit, attend my free one-day training course.'

I was seated on the train, mindlessly scrolling through Facebook, when this charismatic guy with a dazzling set of white teeth and the quintessential Essex charm appeared on my screen. He was a proper 'Essex boy' (Even more than I am). His message was clear and enticing: "Learn how to transform your passions into profit - join me for a free one-day training course." It was my now business partner, Liam Ryan of Assets For Life.

While I had been habitually scrolling past and dismissing his advertisements for weeks, this particular day marked a turning point. It was as if I had finally become receptive to his message, embodying the adage, 'When the student is ready, the master shall appear.'

I soon found myself attending one of his seminars, although I must admit I was initially quite sceptical. It was uncharted territory for me as I had never been to a training seminar before. Moreover,

I had unwittingly developed an ego problem during my successful corporate sales journey, convincing myself that I already possessed all the knowledge I needed.

As the day unfolded, I found myself increasingly captivated, unable to get enough of the valuable insights being shared. Each moment was enthralling, and I was thoroughly enjoying the experience. Then, an enormous opportunity presented itself: Liam was offering personal mentoring for £15,000 plus VAT. I knew this was a chance I couldn't pass up, but there was a problem: I didn't possess the £18,000 required to be mentored by Liam.

I delved deep into my financial resources, investing not only all my available funds across my debit cards but also pushing my limits by maxing out my credit cards. It was undeniably a nerve-wracking decision, as I was essentially putting everything I had into this opportunity. Yet, my intuition strongly insisted that it was a step I had to take. Looking back, I can confidently say that it was one of the most transformative and rewarding decisions of my life.

During this journey, I discovered invaluable skills such as how to be a problem finder as well as a problem solver, how to handle objections with ease and finesse, the art of selling one to many, where I uncovered the potential to earn more in a single day than I used to make in an entire year.

Liam extended me a life-changing opportunity to collaborate in promoting his high-value mentorship programs. This pivotal moment marked the initiation of my journey as an Elite Sales Specialist.

I was able to help people change their lives whilst earning massive commission cheques, it was magical. I also discovered that the more I could learn, the more I could earn. I went on a journey to seek out the best sales experts in the world. I thought I knew how to sell, but little did I know, I didn't have a clue compared to what I was about to uncover.

As my bank balance grew, so did my confidence. I found that people were increasingly receptive to my approach, and my relationships blossomed. I gained the ability to inspire and influence others, and I felt an unstoppable sense of empowerment.

I was living my dream life, and everything was falling perfectly into place.

***

Have you ever experienced a moment in your life when you lay awake at night, filled with a longing to have accomplished more?

Fast forward to December 28, 2021, and I find myself in the Covid Ward at John Radcliffe Hospital in Reading. It's the height of the pandemic, and I'm lying in bed with tubes in my nose and needles in my arms, battling pneumonia.

The lead doctor took me for a CAT Scan. Upon receiving the results, he delivered a sobering message: "Nicholas, I'm sorry to inform you that your lungs are the most severely affected on this ward. We will do everything in our power to help."

At that time, I was only 29 years old, in the prime of health, and a non-smoker. It's a surreal experience to be told that your lungs are in the worst condition among all the patients on the ward. I was so scared.

As I lay on that plastic-laminated bed, wrapped in a thin, itchy sheet, the greatest fear haunting my thoughts wasn't the fear of dying; it was the overwhelming sense that I hadn't made the most of my life.

Despite my numerous accomplishments, there was a significant void in my life, a sense of unfulfillment stemming from not having given back. It struck me that if I were to leave this world, all the knowledge, systems, and processes I had amassed would vanish with me.

At that moment, I made a solemn promise to myself. I whispered, 'Nick, if you pull through this, you'll do everything within your power to give back and share your skills and knowledge with others.'

I then closed my eyes, I was gripped by an overwhelming fear, not knowing if I would ever open them again, I didn't know what was going to happen.

I'd like to express my heartfelt gratitude to the incredible NHS, who stood by my side during this challenging experience and helped me fight through it.

True to my promise, the moment I left the hospital, I channelled 100% of my time, resources, and energy into a new endeavour – writing my first book, 'Selling Is Serving'. This book eventually achieved best-seller status in 21 different categories upon its release. Drawing from all my sales expertise, I distilled it into a straightforward 7-step Elite Sales System that anyone could easily follow to sell with unwavering confidence and conviction.

Following the success of my book, I embarked on a new venture – the 'Elite Sales Bootcamp.' This intensive three-day program was designed to impart my Elite Sales System to as many as thirty business owners each month. From every Bootcamp, a significant portion, typically around eight to ten entrepreneurs, saw the value and chose to invest in an Annual Mentorship with The Elite Sales Academy. This mentorship allowed for a more profound, personalised journey where I could provide hands-on guidance and support, fostering real magic in their sales endeavours.

My most significant source of motivation stems from my unwavering commitment to serving others and fulfilling the promise I made on my deathbed, a promise I was fortunate enough to awaken from in late 2021.

In the words of Richard Branson, 'There is no greater thing you can do with your life and your work than follow your passions – in a way that serves the world and you.' I consider myself truly blessed to have the opportunity to impact thousands of lives by sharing my passions and helping individuals achieve their goals.

One of the most significant challenges I encountered on my journey was the well-intentioned scepticism of my loved ones. They often expressed concerns like 'Maybe now isn't the best time.' or 'Are you sure about setting up events during the pandemic?' It wasn't out of malice but rather their way of looking out for my well-being.

Entrepreneurs are wired to make quick decisions, guided by intuition rather than conventional wisdom. They determine the course of their lives, refusing to be swayed by the opinions of others.

I'm immensely proud and humbled by the growth of my business and the opportunity to pen an impactful book. Furthermore, I'm grateful for the chance to showcase the inspiring journeys of my exceptional mentees, who now have the platform to motivate others facing similar challenges to take action and master the most crucial skill in both life and business – sales.

I sincerely hope you find value in this book, and we'll cross paths at one of our in-person or online training events in the near future.

Remember, if I can do it, so can you.

Thanks,
Nick Staab
Elite Sales Academy Founder.

My Top Tips:

Tip 1: Do everything within your power to avoid negativity at all costs. Stop watching the news, and be careful who you surround yourself with. As Jim Rohn says, 'You are a product of the five people you hang around the most', so if you hang around five broke people, you are going to be number six, hang around five negative people, and you will be number six, perhaps you currently find yourself in the company of five average individuals, and this might be contributing to a sense of mediocrity in your life. If your aspiration is to achieve success and become the best version of yourself, then make a deliberate effort to be in the presence of five successful individuals who challenge and inspire you to elevate your own game.

Tip 2: Recognise the profound significance of mastering the art of sales, for it is a transformative skill that transcends the boundaries of business, permeating every facet of our lives. In truth, life itself is a perpetual series of sales endeavours. Whether it's persuading individuals to embrace our products and services, exerting influence to motivate action, or even coaxing children to consume their vegetables, each of these scenarios involves the fundamental act of selling. Dedicate yourself to honing this skill, and you will witness a remarkable enhancement in all aspects of your life.

Tip 3: In life, there is no winning or losing; instead, it's a continuous cycle of winning and learning. True "loss" only occurs when you persist in repeating the same mistakes despite knowing that you should have taken a different path to avoid them. Prioritise self-investment, as you are your most valuable asset. Embrace opportunities whenever they arise, for the last thing you want is to depart from this world burdened by the weight of unfulfilled potential and unexplored possibilities.

CHAPTER 2

C.A.N.I. - Constant And Neverending Improvement

DIANE MORTON

'I am not a product of my circumstances. I am a product of my decisions.'

- Dr Stephen R. Covey

In simple terms, this quote has encouraged me to have empowering thoughts and ideas; to believe that my past doesn't define me or my future, giving me a new belief that I can create a life that aligns with my greatest aspirations by recognising my strengths and having the resilience required to make new empowering choices, leading me towards a fantastic future filled with limitless possibilities.

I am excited to tell you I am now on that journey.

But it wasn't always like this…

Let me take you back to the year 1972. You see, even when I was young, only seven years old, I didn't have any confidence or belief in myself.

Childhood is a crucial period for the development of core beliefs and early fears, as this is when we form our foundational understanding of the world and our place in it. Traumatic and highly emotional events around my dad's drinking episodes during my childhood contributed to the formation of deep-seated fears and beliefs that followed me into adulthood.

It felt like it was imprinted into my DNA that I wouldn't ever amount to much and that I should just accept my life as average and be grateful for it.

Coming from a very affluent part of Essex called Danbury, I lived in what seemed to me the only council house in the village.

I grew up with stories that enhanced beliefs such as 'money doesn't grow on trees', 'you have to work hard for your money', and it's better to be lucky than rich! LUCKY! RICH! I'd have loved either, and why couldn't I have both, I wondered?

My Dad loved a drink, and although he worked full time and my Mum always had at least two jobs, holding on to money was like trying to fill a bath with the plug pulled out!

Studies have shown that children quite often grow up and find a life partner, wife or husband who mirrors their childhood experiences of their parent's behaviours.

So.... I met and married Rick, someone who loved a drink!

However, added to that, he was also extremely jealous of me, and our early times together were turbulent, to say the least.

I loved him so much but could never reason with him and make him believe anything I ever told him. Being portrayed as a liar massively impacted me. I was walking on eggshells in a constant atmosphere of anxiety and fear, always on edge, afraid of doing anything that may trigger his jealousy and set off his insecurities.

It was exhausting and emotionally draining, and it had a profound and negative impact on me as a person at that time.

Feeling terrified is an emotion that pierces the soul and paralyses the mind and body at the same time. Thoughts become a chaotic storm, like a suffocating blanket of dread, making it difficult to breathe.

Time is stretched out into agonising slowness, as if the moments that follow are an eternity, yet at the same time, everything seems to flash before your eyes, and in this moment of helplessness, rationality seems to slip through the fingers, leaving you in the grips of fear of the *what if's* and worst-case scenarios.

Sadly for me, this became my reality the fateful day that my very drunk husband decided it would be a good idea to get the chainsaw out in the kitchen and cause absolute chaos, turmoil, hysteria and mayhem!

My husband's reckless behaviour with a chainsaw in the kitchen that day posed a real and immediate threat to my and my children's safety and well-being. The sheer terror and helplessness I felt during this event was a culmination of the fear and stress I had already been experiencing for many years in our relationship.

However, this became the straw that broke the camel's back. It became a pivotal moment for me, and I decided to finally take back control of my life for the first time in what felt like forever.

I felt like my survival was in imminent danger; it was an incredibly harrowing experience. It's a sensation that pierces through your every thought and emotion, enveloping you in a thick, suffocating feeling of dread. In that moment, every rational thought seems to slip through your grasp, leaving you at the mercy of fear's grip.

I felt that to survive with my life, I had no alternative but to take massive action.

This event empowered me to seek help immediately. I went to the police, and they found a secure location to protect myself and my children from harm. It was a Domestic Violence Shelter.

The Women's Refuge played a vital role in empowering me to break the cycle of abuse and start to rebuild my life, offering a place of solace. I was able to regain control over my circumstances and start the journey toward healing and independence. It is a critical support service that provides a safe haven for women and their children who are facing domestic violence, abuse, or other forms of intimate partner violence. These shelters offer a secure and confidential environment where women can seek refuge from abusive relationships. They provide not only a physical sanctuary but also emotional and psychological support, legal assistance, and access to resources like counselling. For me, it was a great stepping stone towards safety, setting boundaries, and finding my voice, ultimately leading to positive changes in my life so I could finally become brave enough to break free from the harmful situations that I had found myself in.

I am very proud to say to this day I am no longer a victim, I stand up for what is the truth. I found my voice, and I am not afraid to use it for good.

I found the tools to empower myself to value myself for the first time.

Luckily, the mind has a great way of protecting us by deleting finer details of any traumatic event, blurring the memory enough to allow us to move on in our lives.

Rick got professional help and is now in a place where he no longer engages in any form of bullying or controlling behaviour towards me. This transformation has contributed to a significant shift in our relationship dynamics. By seeking professional assistance, he gained insights into his actions and has learned to manage his emotions and impulses more effectively. This change has created a safer and more respectful environment, allowing me to regain a sense of control in my life. I now feel more empowered to make my own choices, express my opinions and needs, and live without the constant fear or pressure that comes with being in a controlling or abusive relationship. It's been very important for me to continue monitoring the situation to ensure that these positive changes last and that my well-being remains a top priority.

Love is not like a tap; you can't just turn it on and off, and I loved Rick from the bottom of my heart. I felt like he was also a victim in all of this, as I class jealousy as an illness; there are certainly no winners, only suffering in its presence.

Many of you reading this will be very surprised to know that we got back together and are still together to this day. Forty years as I write this chapter. However, the big difference in our relationship now is that I have set boundaries, and he knows I am with him because of love and choice, not fear.

I am very proud to say that the ripple effect of my actions has led him to become not only a great husband but a great dad and grandad, too, and as a family, we are all very proud of him.

***

I'm sure, for many, like me, lockdown came as a massive shock; however, it gave me the time to get clarity in my life and work out what was really important to me and how I would like to impact the world. It led to a very positive change in my career.

Often, challenging situations can become catalysts for personal growth and transformation. My "lightbulb moment" represented a significant turning point in my journey.

Realising the importance of empowering and inspiring others to stand up for themselves, find their voice, and pursue a fulfilling life is an impactful mission. My own experiences and the strengths I've developed serve as a beacon of hope and guidance for others who may be going through similar challenges. My desire to help people lead lives they are genuinely excited about waking up to is a powerful goal. By sharing my story, knowledge, and support, I wanted to make a meaningful difference in the lives of those who may need it most, turning adversity into a force for positive change in the world. My journey from a place of fear and control to one of empowerment and purpose in the world is MY WHY, and that was the reason that made becoming an empowerment mindset coach non-negotiable.

So I set to work…

I spent thousands of pounds and hundreds of hours investing in myself and my skill set, learning to be a Life Coach and NLP practitioner.

It was a great moment when I got all of my qualifications after training for just over a year overall. I was so proud of myself until I realised that I didn't have any clients to empower or even the know-how of sales to get clients.

Money was becoming a challenge for me, too, by this point, as I had poured so much into my education. However, I knew this was a smart move in the long run because nobody can take your knowledge away from you; as they say, it's not what it costs you, it's what it makes you ROI (return on investment), and I was 100% behind my choices.

When you are faced with financial hardships, it can go either way: sink or swim.

You can fall into a hole, but you can't fall out; you have to climb out! That is exactly what I did. I was hungry for success, and I wasn't about to stop there; my only option, at that time, was to get a solution so I could move forward and monetise my knowledge and do it quickly.

My search for a mentor was over, I found an online webinar about sales and how to get the skills required to sell high-ticket products and services to other people. It was like Christmas had come early in the shape of Nick Staab. My gut feeling was telling me there was something special about this guy.

Listening to my heart and being an action taker, I got myself onto his 3-day bootcamp. It was his first bootcamp, and he poured himself into delivering the best event ever.

I was so impressed that when it came to a much bigger investment to work closely with Nick and be mentored by him for a whole year, even though I had no available money, I did something that felt very reckless to me at the time, as it was something I had never done before, I put thousands of pounds on a credit card with no idea of how I was going to pay it back, that's how much faith I put into him and myself to get results.

This was the very first time I had gone all in. In all previous courses I have done, apart from coaching that at the time I could afford, I had just dipped my toe in the water and then tried to figure the rest out alone. That hadn't worked, and as Albert Einstein said, 'The definition of insanity is doing the same thing over and over again and expecting a different result.' So, I took the brave step into the unknown.

If you're anything like me, when you pay, you certainly pay attention, and this is exactly what I did. It's all about taking massive action, I implemented every piece of advice given and very soon started getting paid clients and working for Assets For Life, selling for them at events.

At the Assets For Life Awards Ceremony and Christmas Party combined for the same year, I even won an award. I had been on my way, and I was now an Award Winning Entrepreneur, I had by then learnt another valuable tip: it's all about how you position yourself in the market as a specialist, not a generalist. By the way, up until that day, I was 57 at the time. I had never been to an Awards Ceremony or worn a long dress, and even though my dress was from the charity shop, it was a designer label with hand-sewn beads. I had so many compliments, and I felt like a million dollars.

Today, I am in a very different place from my humble beginnings.

I now divide my time between doing jobs that lift me up and massively helping people too.

Empowering people to unlock their full potential in both life and business resonates with me so deeply, as it was something that eluded me in my own life for so many years. Now, I am on a new and very rewarding mission, not just in monetary terms but also through having the satisfaction that I am making a difference to people's lives on a daily basis, too.

My life has transformed down an exhilarating new path filled with purpose, passion, wealth and happiness.

I work as a Business Training Advisor for one of the UK's Biggest Business Mentors, Adam Stott, selling his high-ticket coaching programmes. This is immensely rewarding not only because it is very lucrative but also because it gets clients the help they desperately need to succeed in business themselves.

This position has been directly linked to the invaluable guidance, training, coaching and mentoring I have been so fortunate to receive from Nick and now also The UK's number 1 Success Coach, Ross Temple. I have been truly blessed and can't thank them enough.

I would like to share a valuable lesson I have learned along the way that has been a fundamental one for my personal and professional development. I have found that Investing in a Coach for myself has been massively important for my continuous learning, and seeking guidance from those who have more experience or knowledge in a particular area has proved to be a game changer. Recognising that I don't know what I don't know is the first step toward growth and improvement. Having a mentor or coach provides valuable insights, accountability, and a structured path towards my success. The benefits of seeking guidance and finding out what I don't know have been a critical factor in keeping me from feeling stuck and in a state of uncertainty or stagnation. The guidance and knowledge offered by my coaches and mentors have been a catalyst for my personal and professional triumphs.

The phrase that Nick Staab uses, '*Selling is Serving*', is so true in this instance. It is also very apt for my own Coaching Programmes that I offer.

They are designed to help and support clients embark on their own empowerment journey of self-discovery and find their voice so they can turn their fears into courage and turn self-doubts into positive beliefs that can help them in everyday life. Embracing the wings of change and possibilities can finally unlock the full potential that may have been lying dormant inside them for many years.

Crucial mindset shifts, becoming aware of their stumbling blocks, and learning how to change routines and habits can be the most rewarding thing in the world, taking them to a place where they are living a life they are truly happy and excited to wake up to and rekindle the flames of the belief that anything is possible!

My future looks brighter today than ever before.

I have also recently become a Psychology and Confidence Mentor for Nick Staab's Elite Sales Academy, offering guidance, support and motivation to those who need it by using my toolkit of Coaching, NLP (Neuro-Linguistic Programming) and CBT (Cognitive Behavioural Therapy) Training skills.

Another thing I am currently exploring is finding new ways of delivering my message so I can impact more lives by speaking one to many on stages and online. At the same time, I have just launched a new Facebook Group, Beyond Addiction Community - Thrive Alive Together, aimed at supporting and helping anyone who is recovering from any kind of addiction to help them get the winning mindset required to be successful in life. Often overlooked, mindset is one of the fundamental building blocks, responsible for 80% of success in life.

In fact, this is backed up by Tony Robbins, who famously said, 'The most painstakingly crafted plans are useless if we can't manage to act on them.'

Tony then goes on to say that success is achieved through a plan that is 80% psychology and 20% strategy; first of all, '*your mind needs to be set*'.

Now, he might know a thing or two about business entrepreneurship and sales; he has sold over 15 million copies of his self-help book and over 50 million audio programmes. He has worked with many celebrities and world leaders, including Bill Clinton, Oprah, Pitbull and Peter Guber.

By the way, I haven't yet mentioned multiple streams of income; it is my secret weapon to future-proof my earning potential, and I believe it should be something to be explored by you, the reader, as well. If you are not already doing this, I strongly advise you to look into spreading your bets; don't put all your eggs in one basket, metaphorically speaking.

I have opportunities to use my voice on stages and get paid for it, too, and it is all very exciting, considering speaking is another passion of mine, and I am fortunate to be able to do that, too.

It's fair to say once I found my passions, what lights me up, and I started living my life in accordance with my core values, I found my get up and go. Now I'm going places and meeting people that I thought were reserved for the privileged people in this world who weren't brought up in a council house. My outlook and view of the world have changed so dramatically, and I am thankful to be able to share with you that I no longer hold onto this limiting belief.

DON'T DREAM YOUR LIFE, LIVE YOUR DREAM!

My Top Tips:

Tip 1: It is often said that 'you are the sum total of the five people you surround yourself with.' The idea behind this is that if you surround yourself with people who have positive beliefs, attitudes and behaviours, it will motivate you to focus on your own personal growth and positive mindset, making it more likely you will be successful. however, a cautionary tale: if you hang around negative people, it could have the opposite effect, so choose wisely.

Tip 2: 'The only person you are destined to become is the person you decide to be!' It sounds so simple, yet it also means that who you become is up to you; it all depends on the choices you make each day. My advice would be to DREAM BIG! And if you can perceive it, it's not big enough, DREAM BIGGER!

Tip 3: 'There are two ways to be happier: change your situation or change the way you look at it!' I love this, as changing perspective on any situation can so easily change everything, and it's good to remember that happiness is found in attitude! By shifting the way we perceive and react to situations, we have the capacity to influence our own happiness by taking action in the external world or by cultivating a positive outlook on life.

CHAPTER 3

Selling Through Storytelling: The Power of Page-Turning PR

HANNAH VINEY

'In the orchard of sales, public relations is the hidden gardener nurturing the tree of prosperity.'

- Hannah Viney

Have you ever been in a position where you simply haven't felt heard or understood?

Let me take you back to February 2018 when I was attending a daytime conference addressing the shocking lack of mental wellbeing support for freelancers in the live events and festivals sector. The guest speaker was the tour manager of rock band Linkin Park, who'd spent countless hours on the road touring with the band but was embarrassed he didn't see any signs of lead singer Chester Bennington's suicide coming. It was a career moment I will never forget - both sobreing and yet lit a fire inside me. Behind closed doors, I am now not ashamed to admit I, too, had been struggling after being diagnosed with professional burnout, resulting in anxiety and depression. Here was someone openly talking about a somewhat closeted topic in that sector - I was emboldened by what I'd heard and felt that working for an innovative PR agency at the time, we had clout and creativity on our side to really make a difference. I'd heard my battle cry and wanted to get to work.

Later that evening, at an award ceremony at which multiple clients had won, champagne was flowing, and there were smiles all around. Out of the corner of my eye, I saw my boss hurtle over towards me with a face of thunder. In front of clients, colleagues and respected industry peers, she proceeded to scream at me, saying that I'd been a waste of space, I'd been carried for three years and that I should be grateful to her for giving me the best job I was ever going to have. All stemming, I've now realised in subsequent years, from an insecurity triggered by my confidence to stand confidently and champion talking openly about mental health within the agency. At that moment, I felt hurt, humiliated and disrespected in front of everyone who had professionally mattered to me. The irony that I'd suffered my own diagnosis was a direct result of pouring blood, sweat and tears into her business to keep my department afloat whilst being severely understaffed seemed to totally pass her by...

It was from that moment forward I knew something had to change. I had to take matters into my own hands.

This one life-changing event turned my professional perspective on its head and gave new clarity to communications like never before.

I knew I wanted to ensure that every business could feel seen and heard in the way I had not been that night.

I took the life-changing decision to walk away from the traditional 9-5 and founded my own business, Sycamore Communications. I identified a gap in the live events market - with a high proportion of freelancers working on the most prestigious, high-profile events requiring external communications support but often without the budget to pay for expensive retainer fees. In we came, offering a high-end level of support but at a fraction of the cost by keeping office overheads down and initially employing our own freelancers rather than permanent staff.

Fighting off stiff competition for a sought-after spot in the NatWest Accelerator Hub, the business cemented its pitching credentials, which successfully converted over 37 new clients across its first four years. Within a year, I went from never having considered running a business to managing a team of six creatives.

Just as my Bristol-based agency was really taking off, including being invited to pitch for the Natural History Museum's PR retainer, COVID-19 hit, decimating the events sector overnight; this unforeseen hardship immediately required the agency to expand its services out to start-ups, entrepreneurs and businesses in any industry in order to remain competitively operational. This pivot away from its initial niche, although unsettling, turned out to be a significantly positive turning point. My attendance at one networking event valued at £250 resulted in converting business contracts worth £39,522 – an ROI of over 15,000%!

Three years in, I had the stark realisation that, as a people-pleaser, I was trying to be a jack of all trades and deliver every single marketing, PR and strategic communications service known to man. I was stretching the team too thin, and it was impacting results - ultimately, we were not serving our clients to the very best of our abilities.

We paused, we pivoted, and we perfected PR.

We now had a new vision that spoke loudly to our dream client. The driving force behind propelling the business forward still derives today from a simple mission. The desire to be the most trusted, impact-led PR agency, telling the stories of 100,000 businesses and taking them from a local to the global stage.

Subconsciously, the skill of selling has always been peppered throughout my CV, and it's been the roles themselves that have inspired me to persistently improve and that have shaped my ability to sell. My very first teenage role at Waitrose saw me rapidly promoted from the tills to the tricky Customer Service desk during a hectic festive season thanks to my calm nature, empathetic ear and willingness to people please at any cost. Little did I realise at the time, but this was effectively my first foray into the world of Crisis Communications - a highly sought-after skill in my current PR capacity. Managing an ever-changing scenario, firefighting an escalated issue and ensuring by the end of the interaction with the customer that they are content and the brand has kept its reputation intact.

Skip forward two years, and you would've found me honing my sales skills, acquiring customer sign-ups for life insurance quotes in an Asda milk aisle on the grey fringes of Edinburgh, as the festival itself drew happier crowds in the city centre. By far the toughest sale of my career - planning for death as you pop out for a pint or loaf is hardly a cheery interaction to instigate.

'Penniless' or so it felt as a Cardiff University student saw me turn my hand to charity telesales, working off a provided script that, after hundreds of calls a shift, saw you muttering it word-perfect in your sleep - even after a raucous night at Vodka Revolutions! Even with roles that weren't perhaps your favourite at the time, the saying 'hindsight is a wonderful thing' really does ring true. Although a role that felt soulless, robotic and with no room to build genuine compassion and rapport with clients due to the extreme fundraising targets, it did teach me one valuable lesson. Every dial was one ring closer to the next kind soul who would kindly donate a hefty sum to a genuinely incredible cause. I had to build a resilient, tough skin who didn't take the course language, hang-ups, screaming rants or simple 'No's as a personal attack - they were just a call moving me closer to success.

That is a vital lesson that I have carried through life, both personally and professionally - Never Give Up.

There are two core ways within the profession of public relations in which selling is actually serving.

The first way at Sycamore that we aim to serve our clients is instilled in the first conversation we have with them. During a 30-minute Discovery Call prior to them coming on board as a client, we explore their current situation with their business, their strengths and weaknesses within the media, where they feel they need the most assistance from our specialist team, and finally, we ask what success would truly look like to them if we had done our job to the very best of our ability. For some with ambitious goals, it's being on the front cover of a specific magazine. For some, it's the fact that for the very first time, they have a structured PR strategy to follow and implement into their start-up, providing clarity and direction.

For us, it is vital to ensure that when selling any of our PR retainer levels (Local Legend, Media Master or International Icon) stand-alone services or educational courses, we have a thorough comprehension of how best we can add value to that client. Selling a shy client into our top package, which requires the confidence to carry themselves on live broadcast opportunities, would be amiss. It wouldn't serve the client or their brand should they not feel ready for that level of media exposure, nor would it, in turn, serve to showcase our expertise.

The second way we use selling to serve is in our day-to-day provision of PR pitching. Coincidentally, the service itself is actually known within the industry as 'selling in', the art of pitching your client's story or expertise to the media and successfully landing press coverage as a result. Every time we write an email or pick up the phone to suggest running a press release or angle, we are selling the credibility, expertise and reliability of our clients to the journalist. Given the nature of such a fast-paced and pressurised role, as PRs, we serve journalists by feeding them with real stories with a human angle for their genuine journalism.

I am now 12 years into working in public relations. I can tell you, the buzz I get today from opening up a national newspaper on a Saturday morning, with a Marmite-laden crumpet and a piping hot, strong Yorkshire Tea and seeing our clients quote or facing smiling back is just as exciting now as it was the first time I landed a piece of coverage as a junior PR rookie. Knowing behind the scenes the hours it takes of painstaking researching, carefully crafting pitches, liaising with editorial teams and picture desks, writing an attention-grabbing release and securing final approval on all sides in order to get a piece of coverage over the line makes it all worthwhile. Then the selling begins all over again...

Although rather a personal admission here, the hardest challenge that encompasses both personal and professional hurdles I've overcome is that of setting up Sycamore Communications in the first place, leaving agency life where you have the camaraderie of a full office to boost you on tough days and celebrate work wins with you, the comfort that your salary will always be paid regardless, the appointment of clients to you rather than having to seek out new projects... the list goes on but I make my point. Leaving security and jumping headfirst into the unknown is a terrifying yet exhilarating adventure. For me, the terror came from reaching a crossroads where I had to become confident enough in my own skin to hold my head high and slowly rebuild my belief that I deserved to be in the same marketplace as before. I was able to find enough clients to make my fledgling company a six-figure business.

And that I COULD do this on my own.

Typically, creative marketing and PR agencies often fall into the all-too-common trap of directly exchanging time for money through the charging structure of a day rate. Having invested in mentors such as Nick Staab, I have transformed the way we serve clients with a simplified retainer structure that can be scaled effectively without the need for my consistent personal input into every account. Not only does this support my professional, ambitious growth plans as a small, female-led business, but it also frees me up personally.

Having the ability to sell, free from the shackles of traditional means, opens up my horizons both literally and figuratively! Free to travel the world, free to start a family, free to spend time with family members as their days become limited…always with the knowledge that the years spent honing skills, buying sales courses and investing in mentors will be paying me back dividends.

My Top Tips:

Tip 1: People buy from people - so building strong relationships with your target audience is key to your sales success. Whether that be one-to-one or promoting to the masses digitally, ensure that your personality shines through to capture the attention of the next leads.

Tip 2: Work on your personal brand to stand out from the crowd. With more marketplaces becoming more crowded and competitive, establishing yourself as the go-to, credible industry expert will assist in naturally easing your sales efforts.

Tip 3: The customer as always…right. You may say, 'It's 2023, let's update this to "Deserving of Honesty."' Rather than bending over backwards to serve everyone, be confident in expressing when you may not be a perfect fit or if you aren't able to serve them in the required manner. This will instil trust in the honesty displayed.

CHAPTER 4

The Unseen Mentor: The Power of Perspective

NANA PREMPEH

'If you want something you've never had, you must be willing to do something you've never done.'

- Thomas Jefferson

PLEASE ALLOW ME to extend my heartfelt congratulations to you for choosing to commence this enlightening journey through the pages of this book. Your decision to delve into these insights suggests a curious mind and a commitment to personal and professional growth.

As for why you chose this book, there could be many reasons, each as valid as the next. Perhaps you're a seasoned sales professional seeking to refine your already impressive skills, or you may be a business owner eager to boost your sales strategies and results. Maybe this book's title or beautifully crafted cover caught your eye, beckoning you to explore its contents. Regardless of your initial impetus, what is crystal clear is your openness to change and your earnest pursuit of personal success.

Rest assured that the revelations in these pages are forthcoming and will significantly impact your life and career.

The knowledge you are about to acquire has the potential to reshape your approach to sales, service, and, ultimately, success.

Over many years, I have endeavoured to understand the intricacies of human interactions and how these interactions (however small) impact relationships and, consequently, the dynamics of the business world.

I've often been surprised by the remarkable difference in performance and execution, in the achievement of some individuals over others, even when presented with the same set of circumstances and parameters.

If you are anything like me, your curiosity is also piqued, and you're undoubtedly eager to unearth the well-guarded secrets and marked differences in those who succeed. I am looking forward to sharing all that I have learnt.

Firstly, please permit me to introduce myself and provide some context as to why I have shared my knowledge with you.

I began my career as a pharmacist at a leading retail pharmacy chain. I quickly rose through the ranks, managing various-sized retail stores, including one of the largest footprints in London. I have always been dedicated and passionate about customer and patient care.

I am also vehemently dedicated to finding talented individuals with diverse skills and backgrounds and putting them together to build exceedingly successful, high-performing teams. I have done this by creating a sense of purpose, empowering individuals, and giving them a consciousness of their accountability. This, in turn, earned me numerous accolades.

I felt I succeeded in my role and was satisfied with my performance. I had established an individual formula for finding talent and succession that meant I could always create successful new Teams and Great Leaders. I felt a sense of pride and fulfilment through that.

Have you ever found yourself in a moment where the illusion of having it all suddenly shatters, leaving you vulnerable to the unpredictable twists of fate?

Let me take you back to December 24th, 2020, a day that etched profound change into the fabric of my existence. It started innocently enough - I was bustling around, preparing for the joyous chaos of Christmas Day. But underneath the surface of festive anticipation, something ominous was brewing. A persistent pain had quietly nestled within me throughout the week, dismissed as a mere aftermath of a spirited football match I'd played a few days earlier. Ignorance wrapped me in its deceptive cocoon until the pain erupted into a symphony of agony, tearing through my body with unrelenting force.

It was a peculiar pain, foreign and terrifying. The discomfort escalated rapidly, urging me to confront a reality I hadn't anticipated. I was alone in my suffering, silently bearing the weight of an unknown affliction. At that moment, I made a pivotal decision; I decided to confront the ominous unknown and seek help.

Navigating the clinical maze of the Emergency Department, I found myself on a hospital bed, enveloped by the sterile scent of disinfectants and the distant echoes of medical urgency. Wires snaked around me like ivy, connecting me to monitors that displayed erratic patterns - tangible proof of my body's distress. The medical staff, their faces etched with concern, whisked in and out, creating a surreal tableau reminiscent of a dramatic movie scene.

Soon, I found myself being wheeled towards the intimidating mouth of a magnetic resonance imaging (MRI) machine. The cold, metallic apparatus loomed over me, promising answers hidden within its depths. With a sense of trepidation, I underwent the scan, feeling a rush of contrast dye coursing through my veins like a lifeline. Back in the stark hospital room, wires once again tethered me to the reality of my fragile mortality.

The verdict was delivered with a gravity that resonated through the sterile walls of the hospital room: I had a blood clot in my lungs. It was a silent assailant, a threat that had stealthily invaded my body, seeking to snuff out my vitality. Immediate treatment became my lifeline, a beacon of hope amidst the shadowy uncertainty.

As I lay on that uncomfortable plastic-laminated bed, wrapped in a thin, itchy sheet, a profound realisation washed over me. It wasn't the fear of imminent death that gripped my thoughts; it was the stark awareness that life, with all its unpredictability, was a precious gift. The fear wasn't of leaving this world; it was of leaving it with dreams unfulfilled, of not maximising the boundless potential that lay within me. This moment of vulnerability became a catalyst, propelling me towards a future where every breath was cherished, every dream pursued, and every day embraced as a precious opportunity for fulfilment and service.

I promised myself that once I was discharged from the hospital, I would make the necessary changes to my life to make my previous ambitions a reality.

Now that you have had a glimpse into my background and the terrain we're about to navigate, you are aware of what it is that motivates me.

Following my recovery, I embarked on a transformative journey of self-improvement. This quest led me to the profound teachings of Assets for Life, a sanctuary of knowledge where I delved into numerous enlightening property programs. Amidst the crowd, a man named Nick caught my attention. In our conversation, his eyes gleamed with confidence as he shared a transformative opportunity he firmly believed could reshape my life. Intrigued and inspired, I took a leap of faith, uttering a resolute 'yes' that would alter the course of my existence. This pivotal moment marked the beginning of a profound shift, an acceptance of the unknown and a commitment to embrace change. Little did I know that this decision would become the catalyst for unparalleled growth and boundless opportunities, leading me down a path of endless possibilities and self-discovery.

I attended the elite sales boot camp. I was quickly engaged. There was so much content, and Nicks's knowledge was inspiring.

I started off by sitting at the back of the room, but by the second day, I was sitting in the first row. I was blown away. The skill I was learning about had clearly been my missing ability. At the end of the third day, my confidence grew. I wanted to know more. I then joined the academy and started attending the weekly sessions.

Within the academy's nurturing embrace, I discovered more than just lessons; I found a vibrant community of kindred spirits, forging connections that transcended mere friendships. Among these remarkable individuals, I found not just friends but a chosen family. Among them was Matthew - a brother from another mother, as they say - a bond that surpassed the boundaries of blood, becoming a testament to the power of genuine connections forged in the crucible of shared aspirations and mutual respect.

Two months later, I could see a further change in myself. I felt self-assured and had faith in myself. By month three, I was closing for assets for life using my newfound power.

I was helping others start a journey that would improve their lives whilst simultaneously, two weekends each month, earning a quarter of my monthly pay.

Although this was nice, it was never about the money. For me, the game changer was the confidence and understanding of what selling as servicing can do to help change people's lives.

As a big Marvel fan, I always remembered Spiderman's uncle saying: "With great power comes great responsibility". I knew I had found a skill that would help me, whether in a business or a healthcare setting.

I knew going forward, my purpose would be educating, inspiring and empowering people, especially the next generation, making their lives better and, in doing so, making the world a better place.

Today, I am surrounded and guided by remarkable figures: Nick Staab, Liam Ryan, Adam Stott, and the legendary Jim Francis. They aren't just mentors in my professional journey; they are my dearest friends, illuminating my path with their wisdom and support.

Now, let's address an uncomfortable truth, one that I've come to embrace wholeheartedly: we are all, in essence, salespeople. It might sound blunt, but it is a fundamental reality.

The art of selling isn't confined to business transactions; it's woven intricately into the fabric of our everyday lives. From the most mundane routines to the grandest aspirations, selling is omnipresent, shaping our interactions, dreams, and connections. It goes beyond the mere exchange of goods and services, permeating our thoughts, actions, and relationships. We are all, in essence, salespeople, constantly negotiating, persuading, and influencing in various aspects of our lives.

Recognising this universal truth, I harnessed the power of selling-is-serving within the healthcare realm where I practised. How did I bring this transformational skill into a healthcare setting? Let me illuminate the myriad ways I applied this principle to benefit my patients.

Firstly, *effective patient communication*: sales techniques such as active listening, empathy, and clear communication enhanced interactions with my patients, led to better understanding, a level of trust, and an outcome of patient satisfaction.

Secondly, *patient education*: I used sales strategies I had learnt to effectively educate patients about their conditions, their treatment options, and any preventive measures they could apply to minimise or eradicate further symptoms, empowering them to make informed decisions about their healthcare.

Thirdly, *building relationships and trust*: building solid relationships with my patients fosters trust, encourages loyalty, and improves patient retention. Sales principles, such as relationship-building, follow-up reviews and personalised care, can be applied to enhance patient-provider connections.

Next, influencing patient behaviour: sales techniques can help me motivate patients to adopt healthier habits and lifestyle changes. By utilising persuasive communication, goal setting, and behaviour change strategies, I can support my patients in achieving positive health outcomes.

Finally, *collaborating with healthcare teams*: sales skills, such as teamwork, collaboration, and negotiation, are vital in multidisciplinary healthcare settings. Medical professionals can use these skills to effectively work with colleagues, ensuring seamless coordination and comprehensive patient care.

In the unexpected tapestry of my life's narrative, there unfolded a chapter that I hadn't anticipated. Here I was, advising a start-up drinks company whose ethos and products resonated deeply with my values. My role was that of a guide, sharing sales wisdom that could potentially catapult the company into uncharted heights of success. Little did I know this consultancy would transform into an extraordinary opportunity.

The founder of this innovative venture, a visionary with a passion for crafting exceptional beverages, saw the potential in the strategies I proposed. Impressed with the progress our collaboration initiated, he extended an offer that seemed too enticing to ignore. Despite my bustling schedule, he presented me with an invitation that echoed with promise, beckoning me to be part of something remarkable.

Joining this vibrant company, I assumed the position of a Sales Director, a role that would soon become not just a profession but a profound passion. The decision was monumental, for it marked my transition from being a pharmacist, a healer in the realm of health, to becoming a part-owner of a soft drinks company, a steward of taste and innovation. The transition was not merely a shift in titles; it was a metamorphosis of identity, a transformation that expanded my horizons far beyond the pharmacy walls.

This unexpected journey illustrated the profound truth behind the concept that selling is indeed serving. It wasn't just about moving products; it was about understanding the intricate dance between consumer desires and exceptional offerings. As I delved into this new role, I found myself not just selling drinks but curating experiences. Every bottle we crafted, every flavour we perfected, was a testament to our commitment to enhancing lives.

In this role, I discovered the symbiotic relationship between service and success. By genuinely serving our customers by understanding their cravings and desires, we were not just selling beverages; we were delivering satisfaction in every sip. The feedback loop of customer delight fuelled our innovation, pushing us to create flavours that tantalised taste buds and stories that resonated with the heart.

In the kaleidoscope of my journey, the trajectory has taken an exhilarating turn, and I find myself brimming with excitement for the future. My newfound skills, forged in the crucible of sales and service, have not just opened doors; they have unveiled entire pathways towards meaningful impact. The prospect of utilising these skills to serve people and businesses has become my compass, guiding me towards endeavours where the fusion of selling and serving can bring about transformative change.

My vision extends beyond personal growth; it's about catalysing growth in others. I am on a mission to acquire businesses or form partnerships where my expertise in selling as serving can be the cornerstone of our strategies. These ventures will not be mere transactions, but collaborations infused with the ethos of genuine service. I am driven to elevate these businesses and to guide them to new pinnacles of success by integrating innovative solutions that genuinely address the needs of our customers.

In my eyes, the future is a canvas where those equipped with a profound understanding of selling as serving will emerge as the true victors. I envision a landscape where businesses built on principles of empathy, integrity, and customer-centricity will not only thrive but lead the way. This future isn't just a possibility;

it's an inevitability. Those who comprehend that every sale is a service, every transaction an opportunity to enhance lives, will shape the business landscape. Their approach won't just be about profit margins; it will be about building relationships, fostering trust, and enriching experiences.

As I step into this future, I do so with a profound sense of responsibility. The knowledge I've gained isn't just a tool; it's a force for positive change. I am not just an entrepreneur; I am a steward of service. Armed with the wisdom of selling as serving, I am prepared to sculpt a future where businesses aren't just entities driven by profit but compassionate ecosystems where the genuine well-being of customers is at the core.

This vision isn't just a dream; it's a roadmap. With every step, I am propelled by the belief that selling is indeed serving, and those who recognise this truth will not just navigate the future; they will shape it, leaving a legacy of meaningful connections and transformative impact.

***

In conclusion, my journey from a seriously ill pharmacist recovering in a hospital bed to a sales director of a soft drinks company I am also a partner in has been a testament to the transformative power of resilience, mentorship, community, and the philosophy of selling as a service.

I invite you to carry these lessons with you on your journey, whether it leads you to the boardroom, a stage, or any other destination. Remember that your path may be unconventional and your challenges daunting, but with unwavering commitment and a heart dedicated to service, you can achieve greatness.

The philosophy of selling as a service has a remarkable ripple effect. When we approach our interactions, whether in business or in life, intending to serve others, we create a positive cycle of empowerment and transformation.

It's not just about the sale; it's about the impact. Every solution we offer and every challenge we help overcome has a ripple effect that extends far beyond the immediate transaction. It touches the lives of individuals, families, and communities, and it contributes to a world where service is the currency of connection.

Embrace the philosophy that selling is not just a transaction; it's a service—a force for good that uplifts, empowers, and transforms lives. And in doing so, we may leave a positive imprint on the world, one interaction at a time.

I believe that the future of selling is indeed serving. As we progress, ethical sales practices will become the norm rather than the exception. Customer-centricity, AI, and emotional intelligence will be pivotal in shaping the sales landscape. Companies that prioritise service and authenticity will not only gain the trust and loyalty of their customers but also enjoy sustained growth and success.

Whether you are a sales professional or a business leader, embracing the philosophy that "Selling is Serving" is not just a choice; it's a strategic imperative. The future will belong to those who understand that by genuinely caring for customers, providing value, and approaching sales as a service form, they can create a better world for all stakeholders, one ethical sale at a time. The ripple effect of this transformation in sales will extend far beyond the bottom line, impacting individuals, businesses, and society.

So, chin up, my friend, embrace sales because the world's waiting for you to take it by storm. And when you do, remember that selling, in all its forms, can be a powerful force for good—a service that uplifts, empowers, and transforms lives.

I trust that my journey serves as an excellent inspiration for you to embark on your path towards greatness. Remember, you are the world's most extraordinary secret, patiently awaiting the moment of your revelation. Your unique talents and potential are like hidden treasures, eager to be unearthed and shared with the world.

> *'If you don't build your dream, someone else will hire you to help them build theirs.'*
>
> - Tony Gaskins

My Top Tips:

Tip 1: First and foremost, I've learned that resilience is the bedrock of transformation. Life will throw challenges at you, some of them seemingly insurmountable. But it's in those moments of adversity that you discover your true strength and potential.

Tip 2: Secondly, mentorship and community are pillars of support that can elevate your journey. Surround yourself with individuals who inspire you and guide you and seek out a community that shares your values and aspirations.

Tip 3: Thirdly, the philosophy of selling as a service is a transformative force that can impact your business and your life. When you approach every interaction with the intention of serving others, you create a positive ripple effect that extends far beyond the transaction.

CHAPTER 5

You're Never Too Young, You're Never Too Old

STEPHEN MURRAY

'Envision beyond the obvious- so don't mine for gold, sell the shovels. Find prosperity in providing solutions rather than chasing a common goal.'

- Stephen Murray

This is a quote I have tried to live my life by when I started my business journey off the back of finishing school last year. It is a simple yet powerful quote that could take you from being the unknown to becoming the unforgettable.

It changes your complete perspective by getting you to look at the bigger picture and not focusing too much on the finer details of things. It is the concept of working smarter, not harder, as you think outside the box, looking at the bigger picture, and finding that need that would most benefit people.

Hence, rather than putting your blood, sweat and tears into mining for the gold, fill the need of selling the shovels to those people, guaranteeing you a result with much less effort.

This quote is what gave me the purpose behind what I will share with you and ties in with my life purpose. My vision in life is to become the best version of myself, achieving all my life goals of becoming a multi-millionaire by just 25 years old.

In doing so, I can then best serve those around me and inspire the younger generations to strive to be the best.

My motivation comes from the belief that anyone can achieve their version of success as long as they have the right belief, they master the skills of sales, and they build a network of the right people. And that is why it's my mission to help business owners live a life of time and financial freedom, where they can do what they want when they want.

Now, some of you may be asking who I am and why I have the right to tell you this. My journey into the world of business and sales started last August, a week before I got my A-Level results.

Now, school wasn't the best time for me at all. Just a bit of a backstory: I was always the shy guy in the back who just went along with everything and never voiced my opinion. I was never the best at school and always saw myself as the most average Joe guy you will ever meet.

I didn't feel lucky enough to be one of those kids who was born with a natural talent or would just excel at things easily. So, as a result, I always compared myself to everyone else, especially when it came to abilities required in school.

Because of this, I never had any confidence, to the point where I was so socially awkward around people, I couldn't even have a normal conversation with someone without making it weird.

This made school life very hard for me, and so I grew up without ever fully experiencing the fun life of being a kid. All of this just caused me to feel depressed, as I was always the outsider who just wandered from group to group and could never fit in.

Thanks to this, I made a bad decision in life and turned to comfort eating, where I developed an eating habit and became overweight, thinking this would make life easier for me. In reality, it did the complete opposite, as I became seriously self-conscious and missed out on countless opportunities because of it!

It also caused me to dread getting up in the mornings, knowing school would be the same all day, every day.

Let me transport you back to the most pivotal moment in my life, the last day of my first year of A-levels. It was meant to be a fresh beginning, a blank canvas filled with infinite possibilities. Despite the 6th form being in the same building blocks as my previous school, I went into my A-Levels with the intention of being the new me.

But this was not the case!

It turned out to be the darkest chapter of my entire existence, my personal rock bottom.

Picture this: I was battling a relentless depression, carrying the weight of my own misery like a heavy burden. Quite literally, I had reached my peak weight of 17 stone, and that only exacerbated my struggles.

At the time, it seemed like there was a correlation between my age and how much I weighed. I was trapped in a body I didn't recognise, constantly haunted by self-consciousness that gnawed me out day in and day out.

My life felt like an endless tunnel of despair, with no glimmer of hope on the horizon. Ambitions and goals? They were distant memories, replaced by a chatter of negative self-talk that echoed in my mind, relentlessly tearing me down.

'You'll never make it.'

'You're just a failure.'

'Why are you even trying?'

These words became the soundtrack of my life, a playlist of self-doubt on repeat. It felt as if this dismal existence was my destiny, a never-ending loop of hopelessness. But little did I know that this moment of despair would be the catalyst for a remarkable transformation, a story of resilience and redemption that I can't wait to share with you.

But then that's when things took a turn for me, and not the normal downward turn. Things started to look up for me. All when

I kept seeing this advert everywhere. Now, I don't know about you, but the moment an advert comes on, I switch off and just wait until the skip button comes up.

That is exactly what I did for the first few weeks. However, my curiosity was piqued when I stumbled upon numerous Instagram videos where individuals spoke passionately about how the book had empowered them to believe they could achieve anything and be successful in business.

Now, considering myself as someone who wasn't particularly into reading, the name of this book clung to my head like a catchy tune you just can't shake.

If you haven't guessed, the book was 'Rich Dad Poor Dad'!

So, after it had been drilled into my brain, I finally gave in and requested the book for Christmas that year. As I delved into the pages, meticulously taking notes- thanks to my very analytical mind, even just within the initial chapters, a profound realisation dawned on me. It was as if the wisdom from those Instagram videos had sprung to life in those written words.

For the first time in my life, a newfound confidence surged with me, transforming my sense of control, and banishing the looming clouds of hopelessness. It felt like a switch had been flipped within my mind, shifting me from a bleak outlook to one brimming with hope and ambition.

With this newfound determination, I declared, 'Enough is enough'. I embarked on a journey to shape the life I truly deserved, a life I had only dreamed of until then. And over the course of a year, I shed an impressive four stone in weight. As the pounds melted away, so did much of my self-consciousness, paving the way for a newfound self-assuredness that enabled me to talk to people effortlessly. It was as if my life was on an upward trajectory, mirroring the rise of a stock chart.

My addiction to self-improvement and success led me to accumulate a library of success and business books. I distinctly recall my 18th birthday, when my friends had parties and bought new watches, where I kept my focus on getting more and more books to path my way to success.

Now, I understand that might make me sound like the 'nerdy one' of the group, but once I got the exhilaration of what my future held, I was wholeheartedly committed to doing anything necessary to work towards it.

My days were consumed with learning, from seizing every free period to absorbing knowledge during regular lessons. I was entrenched in YouTube videos, immersed in books, and enraptured by podcasts, absorbing every nugget of wisdom I could find to pave my path to success.

People around me began to question my sanity, still clinging to the belief that good grades were the sole ticket to a prosperous life. Yet after reading these books, I could now see through the matrix' design, recognising that it was engineered to keep individuals toiling until their last breath.

Reading 'Rich Dad, Poor Dad transformed my mindset, liberating me from the victimhood mentality I once felt.

I became devoted to my pursuit of the life I had envisioned for myself.

Taking a giant leap forward, I began attending online seminars, hungry for every opportunity to further enrich my understanding and expand my horizons.

But amidst all the highs I had been feeling, there was that heart-stopping moment at the end of the seminar when they finally unveiled the cost of entering their life-transforming programme.

You know that feeling when your stomach contracts, the anxiety grips you like a vice, and your parched mouth betrays your inner turmoil. It's that adrenaline rush of frustration, as you just know that the opportunity is slipping through your fingers because you don't have the money.

You just sit there as the chance for a life-altering transformation falls just beyond your reach.

I found myself ensnared in this tormenting moment, not once, but maybe four or five times. Each encounter became more and more painful as questions started to gnaw at my soul: could I truly forge a path to success? Was my dream attainable?

Yet amidst all the struggle, a resolute blazed within me. It was more than a desire; it was a must as I had the biggest drive and motivation ever, with the purpose of retiring my parents.

Witnessing my father's body, battered, and worn out from 35 years of brutal, physical labour just to provide for my family and me, only heightened my sense of urgency.

The fear of whether he would make it to retirement age, still strong and intact, weighed heavily on me. It was this fear and sense of 'now or never' that fuelled my ambitions.

See, I knew that success wasn't merely a wish but instead a necessity, not just for my own future but to gift my father and mother the restful retirement they had so rightfully earned.

Then, one fateful day, I was all set up to watch another Robert Kiyosaki video on the art of real estate investment without having to sink any of your own capital into it.

As I prepared for the video, an advertisement popped up.

I must confess, I was milliseconds away from clicking that 'Skip' button when something insightful caught my ear. The voice emanated from Essex, and the speaker, Liam, was dropping local references like Colchester and Chelmsford- which were places down the road from me and not the other side of the world like usual.

And with a single click, I found myself signing up for Liam's property webinar.

The journey commenced with a meeting with Nick, our enthusiastic guide, who introduced us to Ryan, the master of property courses. But when the moment of reckoning arrived, the pricing revelation sent a familiar chill down my spine. Here I was again, on the steep of another missed opportunity, seething with frustration, cursor hovering over the close button.

But then something magical happened. Nick launched into a sales course, and I instinctively knew this was my gateway to a future full of success. The ability to sell, whether it would be a product or myself, was the key to unlocking the true confidence that had long eluded me.

Without hesitation, I shouted downstairs: 'Mum! Mum! Come look at this?', adamant this was my moment.

Understandably, she was wary, contemplating the use of her credit card for what could potentially be a scam. I passionately explained my plan, assuring her that I intended to invest all the money I had earned from my job at the abattoir with my dad since leaving school.

Moments later, my mother reached out to my father, who initially hesitated, wanting to scrutinise every detail before committing. But I wouldn't relent. I fervently sold the vision to them, conveying that this course marked the dawn of my future. I couldn't bear the thought of missing out on another life-altering opportunity.

After much persuasion, they relented, and I took the plunge. I invested every pound I had saved up for a car, and I enrolled in the closest three-day bootcamp a mere ten days after the seminar.

Looking back, I can confidently say it was one of the best decisions I've ever made. From day one, I was enveloped in a nurturing community of like-minded individuals, all supported by Nick and his remarkable team.

Nick's support and teachings infused me with a newfound support I couldn't have imagined.

They made me realise that my dream life was not only attainable but well within my grasp. It suddenly clicked why I had struggled with conventional schooling - I possessed an entrepreneurial mindset that didn't quite fit the mould.

The traditional path of the rat race, working tirelessly until retirement, didn't resonate with me.

Since hanging around successful, like-minded, but most importantly, driven individuals, I am now further along my business and sales journey than I could have ever imagined at this point. My network has now experienced a significant surge of wealth, to the extent that I now find myself in the company of accomplished multi-millionaires and thriving business proprietors. These encounters opened doors like stepping stones, pathing my way to that congruent future I had always dreamed of.

Currently, I am presented with the opportunity to gain knowledge, engage in sales, and provide guidance as part of one of the UK's leading business coaching enterprises, Big Business Events, where we help thousands of entrepreneurs start, scale, and grow their businesses to the point where they are living the life of their dreams, and they can be working on their businesses rather than it.

I am fortunate to collaborate with the UK's no.1 success coach, Ross Temple, who provides me with daily mentorship, delving deep into ways I can assist others through business and life coaching.

By mastering the art of selling both on the phone as well as in person doing high ticket selling, I am able to personally help these entrepreneurs through the struggles they are going through and help them to start a path down to success, similarly to how I was first guided down a journey through Nick.

Having this newfound confidence has empowered me to seize numerous fresh opportunities, with a particular focus on developing my personal brand.

Now, I can proudly proclaim to the world that I hold the distinction of being the UK's youngest-ever Elite Sales Specialist and one of the country's youngest-ever Neuro-Linguistic Programming practitioners and coaches.

What's more, I've embarked on the exciting journey of public speaking, taking to the stage to share my knowledge with broader audiences shifting from one-on-one interactions to one-to-many conversations. Marking my initial steps towards hosting my own webinars and events all by the age of 19.

My main inspiration and motivation springs from the dread of being enslaved in the rat race my whole life. The idea of working a 9-5 job for six long decades, only to retire with very little to no pension. It's lyophobia.

The fear of regret of missing out on life's true wonders and experiences and lacking the time and financial freedom to really enjoy life to the extent of how it is supposed to be.

But still, to this day, I encounter many challenges on a day-to-day basis.

The biggest is my severe imposter syndrome.

The idea of 'I can't do this because of my age or lack of experience' which sometimes holds me back. But even some of the most successful entrepreneurs out there face the same reality.

One of the biggest is Kim Kardashian, who said she still faces imposter syndrome, but self-doubt keeps her going.

And that's where surrounding yourself with the right people comes into place because they are the ones to guide you through life and want to help each other succeed. Because at the end of the day, you are your own biggest asset, so if you can see the world through that lens, then life becomes much less scary.

Overall, I greatly appreciate the people who have been with me on my journey, no matter whether they are still with me today or they went on their own life path. Everyone I have met and everything I have done has shaped me into who I am today, and I greatly look forward to meeting new people and taking on new, exciting adventures.

And hopefully, one day, I will meet you too!

My Top Tips:

Tip 1: The most crucial aspect of life is developing your personal brand. It's the key to success in life and business. Brand-building isn't solely self-promotion; it's about crafting a consistent, authentic identity that sets you apart. When people anticipate your expertise and hold a favourable perception of you, they'll choose you. It's a potent tool for achieving goals, making a positive impact, and leaving a lasting legacy.

Tip 2: Success hinges on embracing the winner's mindset. As Winston Churchill noted, 'Pessimists see problems in every opportunity, while optimists find opportunities in every difficulty.' You can always find a positive outcome in any situation, no matter how bleak. Whatever life throws at you, you'll emerge stronger.

Tip 3: 'Don't do it alone!' While you've heard this advice frequently, I can't stress enough how vital it is to seek mentorship. What might take years to accomplish alone can be achieved in six months with the right guidance and support. You can't master everything, so why waste time learning when you can tap into someone else's expertise? They've dedicated their life to mastering that skill and can show you the way or do it for you.

CHAPTER 6

Unlocking Your Athlete Mindset

SUZ HAWKINS

'Today I will do what others won't, so tomorrow I can do what others can't.'

- Jerry Rice

My childhood wasn't typical. Now, don't get me wrong, I had a fantastic childhood, and I am grateful for every single moment of it. However, while other children were having sleepovers, I was getting up at 5 am; other kids were having holidays while I was travelling the country with my dad; my friends had the latest toy or piece of technology, and I was mucking out stables and cleaning my equipment.

If you haven't guessed it already, I had horses.

Most of my family had horses in their lives at some point, so it was inevitable that I would follow the trend. However, me being me, I had to do better, and I wanted to be the best. From about the age of 10, I began to show a natural talent, and my parents and coaches decided to see how far I could go in the competitive world of Dressage.

As I progressed up the levels and got invited to join The British Under 21's Squad at 14, things started to get serious. Now, if you think having horses is expensive, try having horses and trying to be the best in the country! I did not come from a wealthy background; my parents were foster carers, and we lived in rented accommodation. We did not own my competition horse, instead she was on loan, and she was a complete novice when I got to ride on her. My weekends, school holidays and mornings before school were spent working for my trainers in exchange for coaching. Competition fees, equipment, transport, and expenses went on credit cards, and we barely kept our heads above water.

With so much at stake, I had to be my absolute best, I had to leave nothing on the table. Every time I competed, there was no excuse for second place. With Dressage, the results were scored in percentage; therefore, the difference between 1st and 2nd place could sometimes be 0.1%. These tiny margins meant I had to be firing on all cylinders and make sure every aspect of my life worked for me to make me the best I could be. We began to monitor my sleep, we ensured my nutrition was on point, and we tracked my water intake. We also made sure that my schedule was streamlined to juggle my studies with competing and training. I genuinely believe managing these lifestyle factors gave me the edge over my competitors when it mattered most.

When I was in my early 20s, I wanted a new sporting challenge and a new skill under my belt. Fitness and competition had to be key as I never do anything by halves! With past personal trainers, we had done some pad work during sessions, and I really enjoyed the discipline and technical side of it.... So, I threw myself into boxing.

For the next three years, my life was spent in the world of boxing. Alongside this, I studied Sports Science at Brighton & Hove and completed an AASE (Advanced Apprenticeship in Sporting Excellence) in Boxing. During this time, I had the chance to fly out on a training camp to Tenerife, where I got the opportunity to complete a half marathon at altitude on Mt Teide, which is still one of the hardest fitness challenges I've ever completed, hands down! In addition, I got an opportunity to box in an international university bout against America. Just like my dressage career, my lifestyle factors had to be on point to perform at my best.

Now, there was a slight flaw with my boxing journey... I wasn't naturally gifted at it! I was slow and got hit a bit more than I would have liked! However, we discovered that I was naturally quite strong, so if I hit you, you were in trouble… it just didn't happen very often!

At this point, I stepped back from sport, fitness, and training. I needed a breather. My life up to this point had been so focused on performance, and it had consumed me, I was tired, had gone stale and had lost the love for it. This lasted about two years until I started to get restless and miss that discipline, structure, and competition buzz.

I didn't know where to start again, and I was lost. I had been out of the game too long to pick up where I left off with the horses, and I knew boxing wasn't for me long-term. So, I decided to join a gym with the first goal of just getting fit again. After a few sessions, that drive began to build again, and I knew I wanted to be the best I could possibly be, so I decided to get a coach. I looked at the profiles of all the trainers, and I was drawn to one in particular - he was the most qualified, he was a master in his field, and he had competition experience, which means he would relate to my motivation. I signed up and got ready for my first session. My coach competed in Strongman, which I knew nothing about other than seeing it on TV as a kid at Xmas. As our sessions went on, my natural strength began to come back and develop, and my weights quickly increased. It was at this point he dangled the competition carrot in front of me, and of course, I grabbed it. I had the bug back, I had that motivation again, and I was ready to start achieving again. I was now going to compete as a Strongwoman.

Now, you may have seen for yourself I don't do things by halves. I am all in, no excuses and I do what's needed to get the job done. So, with this trend, we booked my first competition! It was a qualifier for England's Strongest Woman! Now, this may sound like a terrifying prospect to most; however, for me, the bigger the stage, the better. I love to perform; challenge me to do something, and I will do it, and then some. Luckily, my competitive background meant that I was comfortable under pressure.

Competitions are my playground to show everyone what hard work can achieve, and I know how to get my mindset into the correct state and channel my emotions to work for me. This backed with an amazing coach, and ensuring my lifestyle factors were supporting me, I felt ready. Long story short, I won the Southern Qualifiers and qualified for England's Strongest Woman!

Sadly, I chose not to compete in the finals that year; strength is a marathon, not a sprint, and the weights I would have had to have lifted in the finals, my body just wasn't ready for at that point, and I would have been putting myself at risk of injury. Since then, I have won four out of my five competitions and have/have held the following titles: The Strongest Woman in The South (2 consecutive years running), Double England's Finalist, Essex Strongest Woman, and Horsham's Strongest Woman.

I was back doing what I loved, I was completing, I had goals, and once again, my lifestyle factors were being managed, and I was feeling great. I realised at this point that I wanted to start helping others and pass on some of the knowledge and experience I had gained from my years of training and competing in the three different sports. I decided to invest in myself and become a qualified level 3 personal trainer.

Now, the fitness industry is massively saturated with personal trainers. Some incredible trainers are super experienced in their field, but there are also many school leavers who didn't know what else to do and being a PT seemed like an easy option! I knew I had a lot of qualities and a lot to give, but I needed to stand out and systemise my business. This is where I really needed to focus on my sales.

Since Nick and I got together, I got to see behind the scenes that I came around to the importance of sales. This wasn't an easy task, however! Nick will openly admit that I wasn't the easiest student! However, I soon realised that my previous perception of sales was all wrong; instead, it was all about helping people and solving their problems.

We also quickly realised that the discipline and skills that I had learnt over the years of being an athlete translated really well to people in business. It is now my vision to educate business owners and individuals on the importance of lifestyle factors and how this increases their day-to-day performance and long-term success. How do these tie in? Let me explain 3 of these Lifestyle Factors in more detail:

1. Hydration:

   As our brain is 75% water, Hydration plays a critical role in physical and cognitive performance.

   Poor hydration can impair cognitive function, including concentration, decision-making, and reaction time. In business, where mental focus and cognitive function are key, dehydration may mean you aren't able to handle objections effectively or struggle in an important pitch or client meeting. Even mild dehydration can lead to errors and reduced performance.

Dehydration can lead to feelings of fatigue and reduced energy levels. This can be particularly detrimental during long days or when you have many things to juggle.

2. Nutrition:

Nutrition plays a crucial role in cognitive function, and the foods you eat can significantly impact your brain health and mental performance, energy levels, confidence and how you feel day-to-day.

The brain is a highly energy-demanding organ, accounting for a significant portion of your daily energy expenditure. Our brain is fuelled by glucose, which is extracted from carbohydrates and stored as glycogen in the liver and muscles. This is used as the primary source of energy for the brain. Maintaining stable blood sugar levels through a balanced diet and eating at regular intervals can help ensure a steady supply of glucose to the brain, supporting cognitive function and concentration. This will help prevent energy dips, brain fog and loss of concentration, which can be massively detrimental when trying to run a business or perform at your best in your job.

Certain nutrients, such as amino acids (the building blocks of proteins) and vitamins, are essential for producing and regulating neurotransmitters, which are chemical messengers that transmit signals between brain cells.

Antioxidants (found in fruit & veg), Omega 3 fatty acids (found in fatty fish, walnuts & flaxseeds) and Micronutrients (i.e., B, D, Iron and Zinc, for example) all also play vital roles in preventing cognitive decline, effective communication between brain cells, improved memory, and processing information.

In order to perform at our optimum level, we must ensure that we are fuelling our bodies correctly. If you had a nice car, you wouldn't try and run it on fumes or cheap, watered-down fuel; our bodies are no different. Correct nutrition is not just responsible for our performance today but also plays a key role in our future health and well-being in later years.

3. Sleep:

Sleep plays a huge role in how we feel and how we are able to perform. However, it is something that we don't give enough respect to. Often, it comes down to poor habits or discipline, and just because you think you can get by on 4 hours of sleep a night doesn't mean you should! Sleep helps our minds and bodies in some of the following ways:

- Restoration and recovery of muscles, tissues, and immune system
- Memory consolidation, which is the process of turning short-term memories into long-term memories, is crucial for learning and retaining new information

- Mood regulation, prevention of stress and increased mental health
- Increased reaction times and alertness
- Prevention of degenerative disorders such as Alzheimer's
- Cognitive functions such as decision-making, creativity and concentration

We also need to consider not only the amount of time we sleep but the quality of the sleep we are getting too. When we sleep, we go through 5 different stages of sleep, and we cycle these stages multiple times a night. The length of each stage will vary from person to person, as well as change as the night progresses. It is during the deep sleep of these stages that the body is able to repair and regrow tissues, and energy is restored. The longer we sleep, the more sleep cycles we are able to achieve, therefore increasing our long-term health and overall well-being.

My Top Tips:

Tip 1: Trust the process. Success is not a linear journey; there are highs and lows, and there are struggles and roadblocks on the way. Believe in your decisions, have faith in yourself, and each day, just take that one step towards your goal, no matter how small it may be. Surround yourself with the right people, educate yourself and remember it's a marathon, not a sprint.

Tip 2: Surviving is not succeeding! I speak to lots of people who tell me they can function on three hours of sleep a night or just drink tea all day and that they don't see why they would need to change their habits. Just surviving and getting by each day is not being the best version of yourself; you are not reaching your full potential, and you are putting your body under unnecessary stress.

Tip 3: There are no sexy shortcuts! The health and fitness industry is a multi-billion-pound industry, and remember, ultimately, every product, service and trend has the underlying intention of making money for someone. Sadly, this industry feeds off of our insecurities and pain, and when we are in this position, we want quick fixes with guaranteed results. Products will be packaged in a sexy way with big promises and false claims. Sadly, healthy living and achieving health goals (whether that be muscle building, weight loss or weight gain) is a tough journey which involves discipline, commitment, and hard work. However, the good news is that there is no complex magic formula; it comes down to the simple principle of a healthy, balanced diet and an active lifestyle. When it comes to the health industry, if something sounds too good to be true, then it probably is.

CHAPTER 7

Taking Action Saved My Life

SUZANNE JENKINS

'Upgrade your mind, and you will upgrade your life and have a positive impact on the lives of others around you.'

- Suzanne Jenkins

EVERY CHANGE YOU make in your life will have a ripple effect on others. Inspiration and encouragement can move mountains. Lead by example by being the change you want to see.

I am a positive mindset and happiness coach who loves helping others become the best versions of themselves to live fulfilling, purposeful, and joyful lives by encouraging, inspiring, and supporting them through their journeys. Whilst my focus is not on mental health per se, I firmly believe the service I offer could in some way preempt mental health problems.

Helping others is in my DNA. The results of an archetype profile score me as 60% caregiver, so there are no surprises there. Caring and helping others is something I have always done. From being in the brownies at seven years old, helping to care for Grandparents from around the same age, through being a Sunday school assistant at fifteen years old, to more recently, having 14 years of experience working at Mental Health Charities. The latter came about after a bout of my own mental health issues, of which I am 95% better. Be honest, who doesn't have any problems or bad days?

Let me explain a bit more about what happened to me. I had spent 25 years carving out a career in Finance; I became a qualified Chartered Management Accountant working in several large IT companies. The pay was good, but the hours were long. I did this type of work because I was good at it, and initially, I wanted to, but I did not enjoy it.

In 2008, one of my many tasks was heading up the European division of a globalisation project. My health had become more and more problematic over several months. I had been travelling to the US a lot, working even longer hours, and not seeing much of my family. I had terrible pain in my shoulders, affecting my arm movement, plus my fingers were losing flexibility and getting stuck. In addition, I had pain in my knees and feet, and to top it all, pain in my pelvic area. I was struggling with the physical demands of my job as well as the mental demands.

In short, I was struggling to keep up and keep going.

One day, I went to work and was hardly able to use my keyboard. Then, I tried to get a folder of documents down from a shelf. I had terrible pain in my shoulder and hands, which forced me to drop the folder. I left it where it was, found my boss and told him I was going home as there was something very wrong, and I needed to find out what. I had previously told him of my health issues, so it should not have been a shock to him. However, the look on his face and comments from him implied that it was. I didn't engage with him. I just turned around and walked out.

Little did I know I would never return to the office. Fast forward four weeks, and I was diagnosed with Rheumatoid Arthritis. I was not surprised as some of my family had the same diagnosis. Over a period of two to three months, my physical and mental health deteriorated even further. I was also diagnosed with a fibroid the size of a tennis ball that needed attention. Several weeks later, Morton's Neuroma (inflammation of nerves, cause unknown) in both feet. Both ailments required treatment and subsequent surgery.

I could see a very bleak future as, at every turn, more problems were appearing. I was in complete despair. I saw a future of continual reduced mobility, the prospect of having a hysterectomy, and pressure from work regarding the project. Eventually, I imploded! I started going out in my car late at night on my own (one of the few things I was able to do), tears streaming down my face, wanting to end it all. I would drive at silly speeds down the motorway in the middle lane and just close my eyes.

I wanted to end this constant pain and misery I felt. I was a failure.

Everything about me had been for nothing.

Neither my body nor my mind could deal with my life. What else was going to crop up?

I could not stand it any longer. I wanted out! Despite how I felt, there was always something that pulled me back. I would open my eyes and discover I was on the hard shoulder or about to hit the central reservation and would swerve back to a safe lane. I think the caring side of me kicked in again, always thinking of others. Guilt about if I hurt or killed somebody else, the services to clear up my mess, the impact on my family, etc. Typical me, even in my darkest point, I was putting others first. I can almost laugh about it now.

Anyway, after several attempts, I finally reached out for help and supported by my partner at the time, I managed to get the right help. I was a day patient at a private Mental Health Hospital. I was under their care for about nine months. During this time, I underwent various sessions of CBT (cognitive behavioural therapy), yoga, and talking therapies. They also supported me through both of my surgeries. My main breakthrough was writing a daily gratitude journal. Initially, I could not see the point or see anything to be grateful for. After two weeks of doing this daily activity, I began to feel a slight shift. I could feel a small glimmer of hope, of feeling less miserable.

I continued to make small improvements until I left their care. Once I had left, I felt alone again, with no support mechanism, and I was scared. By chance, a few weeks later, I found a local council-funded day centre run by a local mental health charity.

Relief! I could continue my recovery with people who understood me. Over several months, my mental health improved enough that I started volunteering at the centre. I wanted to give back and help others, too. Volunteering went to subsequently being employed. I initially helped at the craft group, then went on to run a meditation group and a singing group.

The singing group was my favourite as it was always cheerful and uplifting. Everybody seems to love Abba and Kylie's songs. The clients loved all these groups, and the number of attendees grew. I then went on to have my own caseload of clients, which also grew in number over the years as I became more experienced and promoted. One manager encouraged me to write a few workshops they could run. She believed I had the lived experience and knew what worked well. One of the workshops I wrote was also picked up by a local NHS agency and facilitated by myself and my manager. It was six weekly sessions and was run seven times by us on behalf of the NHS Agency. I still wanted to help people more. I wanted to be better at helping.

While doing online research for activities that could help my clients, I came across a wealth of useful websites that pricked my curiosity further. Official qualifications were calling to me. This would give me the structure to increase my ability to help others. I had the passion, so why not? Over the next few years, I invested £15,000 in training in Counselling, NLP (Neuro-Linguistic Programming), Breakthrough Coaching, Hypnotherapy, Time-Line Therapy, and Positive Psychology, each gaining recognised qualifications. During this time, I had a life coach myself for 18 months at a cost of £5,000. The more I learned, the more I could help my clients. I was able to use different methods for different problems my clients were facing, and dependent on what worked for the client, understanding that we all learn and like to do things differently, using the Visual, Audio, Kinaesthetic or Audio Digital preference of each client. Communicating with them in ways that connected with them, ensuring they understood what we were doing and, more importantly, why.

After 14 years, I had outgrown my role at the Mental Health Charity, so I decided to set up on my own as a life coach focusing on Positive Mindset and Happiness and started Zan Life Coaching. For the first time, I was required to get my own clients rather than have them referred by other means such as GP Surgeries, NHS Agencies, or Support Workers. It had been like a conveyor belt of readymade clients.

Going out and getting my own clients was a daunting task for me. I did not know how to go out and obtain clients and sell my service, which was actually selling myself. How do you sell? I had never sold anything in my life except at jumble sales whilst in the Brownies. I thought of all the cold calls I'd received in the past, all the sleazy car salesmen I'd met, you get the picture. I did not want to feel uncomfortable or 'icky' when having conversations with potential clients.

By chance, I saw an ad on Facebook for a free business event which was being held locally. The first presentation was very interesting, but the second was even more so. That was when I came across The Elite Sales Academy. I listened to the presentation by Nick Staab and thought that, yes, this is the way I want to conduct sales. I immediately signed up for his 3-day Bootcamp without a second thought. His ideology about what selling actually meant resonated with me. Selling is serving. You are serving the potential client by selling your service if it is the right fit. It gives them and you the opportunity to discuss their wants and needs to see if your service fulfils that. You are not trying to fit a square peg in a round hole. If it is not a right fit, you can still help them by giving them some value and help, even if that help is pointing them elsewhere.

In May 2023, I attended the 3-day bootcamp. It was fantastic. I learnt a lot about selling as serving, and building relationships with potential clients. I felt like a new woman. After attending the bootcamp, I really did feel much more confident in conducting sales not only to potential clients but also when attending networking events and just generally in life.

I also feel more confident in myself and what I am doing in my business. I have a message to share with the world that is beneficial. I've also signed up for 12 months to The Elite Sales Academy, where I have had the courage to re-write my group programme, the 'Life Mastery Blueprint'. This programme is designed to upgrade your mindset and unlock your full potential to live a more fulfilled and enjoyable life. It is my way of sharing the knowledge I have gained to live a much happier life. How by putting challenges into perspective and seeing them as opportunities to do something differently, or something completely different. To focus on what you can do rather than what you cannot, preparing people to be more resilient to change and how to navigate the curveballs life can sometimes throw your way.

My mindset has changed so much over the years. I have discovered that stepping outside of my comfort zone is not as scary as I used to think. You can overcome problems by looking at them differently and regard them as bumps in the road rather than mountains. You can look at challenges as new opportunities. You can look for the positives in all circumstances, which helps you detach from emotional outbursts and knee-jerk reactions.

Most importantly, you are never too old to learn new things or do new things. Investing in yourself is the best investment you can make. The dividends are priceless, and they change your life for the better. A leopard can change its spots, I am living proof of that. My improved confidence has also led me to participate in podcasts, sell on behalf of other organisations, and be ready to present my signature programme to the world.

I plan to use selling to expand my business to help more people become the best version of themselves. To help others in ways that get phenomenal results. To get people to go from the relative comfort of a group programme to feeling more comfortable diving deeper into a 1-to-1 programme with myself. Here, we can go to the next level to work on limiting beliefs and any other blocks holding them back from pursuing their dreams. We can work on goal planning in more detail and implement more of the activities covered in the group programme into their daily lives.

As someone who has gone from being suicidal to living a fulfilled and enjoyable life, I feel it is my duty to help others either in a similar situation or who are beginning to find life a struggle in some way. I had help, and I wanted to give help to others, too. I have always helped others in some shape or form, and I will continue to do so. It is what I truly believe is my reason for being here and opening my eyes whilst on the motorway.

My vision for the future is to inspire others and bring them hope for an amazing life. Encouraging them to pass on what they have learnt and inspire those around them by leading by example.

Or, put another way,

It is my mission to help individuals develop a clear sense of purpose, unlock their inner strengths, and achieve their full potential.

So, they are empowered to take control of their lives, overcome obstacles, and create meaningful lives for themselves.

Through coaching, inspire individuals to become their best selves and make a positive impact on the world around them.

I cannot thank Nick enough for his support over the last few months. His inspiration, encouragement, and approach to coaching have made one of the most positive impacts on recent life. I look forward to continuing under his mentorship.

What's the saying… 'When the student is ready, the teacher will appear.' Well, here we both are, ready to take on the world.

In closing my chapter, I would like to give you my top three tips. Good luck with your own journeys, and thank you for reading.

My Top Tips:

Tip 1: It is okay to ask for help. Asking for help is not a sign of weakness; it is a sign of strength. It takes courage to show your vulnerability and ask for help. I wish I had asked for help earlier.

Tip 2: Practice gratitude every day. It will change your perception, lift your mood, and make you more resilient when challenges appear.

Tip 3: Become an action-taker. If you want change, YOU must do something to obtain that change.

CHAPTER 8

New Horizons After Retirement

ABIOLA DIKKO

'You have a dream, a purpose inside of you! All you need is someone to help get it out of you.'

- Abi Dikko

My name is Abi Dikko, and at the time of writing this chapter, I am sixty-nine years old. This should be an awesome inspiration to my fellow elderly contemporaries to know that there is no one too old to join the Elite Sales Academy. Actually, there is no one too young, either, to join the Academy. We had a young man join us at the age of eighteen who has had a brilliant journey.

I first joined the Elite Sales Academy in February of 2021, and it has been an amazing journey to date. It certainly was not what I was looking for, nor was it what I expected, however, it has been a very profitable experience for me in very many ways.

I have a Bachelor of Science degree in Pharmacy from 1975 and a Postgraduate Diploma in Primary School Education from 1980. In addition, I have an Advanced Bookkeeping Diploma (from 1997). I have worked in several diverse capacities. For ten years, I practised as a pharmacist. This involved Hospital Pharmacy and research in a Drug Manufacturing Company and also included being a lecturer at university. All of these positions were in Zaria and Kaduna in Nigeria. As my family grew, I spent five years teaching various age groups in a primary school, also in Kaduna, until I moved to England.

Arriving in London, my very first job was working in Marks and Spencer's at the till. It was a pleasant job, but the hours were not suitable for my family, and neither was the pay. I found that to practice as a pharmacist here in the United Kingdom, I would have to complete a refresher course, which would take one year, but with young children, this was not possible for me. I then took on a finance role in the church I attended after I completed my studies in bookkeeping and also managed the church bookshop.

I finally took on the role of the Finance Officer in a High School, also in London, until I retired. I thoroughly enjoyed the diversity of what I was capable of doing until my retirement in 2021, which was just before I turned sixty-seven years old. I also served as an Elder in the Commonwealth Christian Fellowship and still do to date.

I initially enjoyed a couple of months of "freedom" but was not satisfied with "doing nothing". Even though I was fully invested in helping out with the eight (soon to be nine) grandchildren, the children of my four children, I still felt the urge to continue to invest in myself and become profitable. I came across an Assets for Life advertisement, which eventually led to me joining the Elite Sales Academy without any previous background in sales, except for working in the bookshop of my church and my short stint in Marks and Spencer.

In January 2022, having retired six months before, I became restless and was thinking of some part-time work to keep me occupied. I then came across a YouTube presentation by Liam Ryan, advertising a webinar that promoted Serviced Accommodation. This appealed to me because our family had a dormant, well-presented, two-bedroom flat in the family. I immediately booked my place on this webinar.

After listening to Liam Ryan, I decided to try out my hand with the dormant flat. I booked a place on the Serviced Accommodation Boot Camp for March 2022. The webinar was actually a full day of three presentations, which included The Elite Sales Academy pitch by Nick Staab.

Nick mentioned that if we had booked for the Serviced Accommodation Boot Camp, then we would certainly need the sales training to enhance our skills. I, again, immediately booked a place on the Elite Sales Bootcamp. Unfortunately, the dates for my Serviced Accommodation Bootcamp clashed with a family function, and I had to reschedule the Serviced Accommodation Boot Camp for a later date in the year. Therefore, I ended up going to the Elite Sales Boot Camp at the time, which was held in February 2022. And what a surprise I had! It was not at all what I thought it would be.

Previously, my thoughts about sales conjured up one of two pictures; the first was selling goods in a shop, and the other was attempting to sell over the phone or by cold calling at someone else's door.

But since joining the Elite Sales Academy, I have come to realise that, no matter who we are or what we do, we are actually selling all the time! We constantly sell our 'point of view,' or 'our way of life' or even 'our goals and our convictions'.

To me now, 'Sales' is not just about selling products but, more importantly, about serving others. i.e., how I can make someone else's life better through the knowledge and the expertise that I have gained in life or even by the product that I sell. There is always a joy in bringing satisfaction to a 'customer'. I now realise that the objections others make when presented with a sale are just a way of seeking to be reassured of the decisions that they will make. We get to listen to what clients are saying, and then we are able to suggest the best available solution for them to achieve their goals.

Each person in the Sales Academy is encouraged to pursue their dreams or the vision that they have inside of them. We have been given very practical ways of continually moving forward. We are always learning! The mentors are on hand to help you when you get “stuck”. We have been introduced to Systems, which we are able to develop personally according to our own specific area of expertise, which, when followed closely, brings us to our expected end.

One thing that changed my personal way of thinking was using my credit card as leverage for what I was investing in without having to raise the finances first. This was great motivation for me to work hard at what I was being taught in the Academy, knowing that there would be great returns at the end of it all to pay off my credit card. In the past, I always felt that I had to pay off my credit cards at the end of the month.

My mindset has completely changed about sales and, actually, about myself.

I have always had a passion for cooking African food, and the people around me loved my food! After having a few sessions at The Elite Sales Academy, this came to light, and I was encouraged to turn it into a business.

It has now become a fully registered Food Business, even though I only cater for family and friends at present (this is actually all I can cope with, as I do everything myself, which I absolutely enjoy). It brings in sufficient income to meet all of my needs without the need to spend my pension. It also has growth potential; however, it has been my decision to keep it small until one of my family members is able to join me in the business and run with it. I have a vision to pass the business down to generations to come and will do so in the near future.

At one of the Academy Days, held every three months, we had a guest speaker called Phil Elder. He spoke about how he began to have multiple streams of income and about how to let your money work for you instead of working for money.

From an idea that would come up, he would turn it into a stream of income. I was so inspired by his talk and was determined to do something about it. I sought out investments for my savings and my pension, which I was hoping to just allow to grow and leave as a legacy for my grandchildren, but I have since found a great cause to invest the money in, and now my money is working for me and earning more for me than I earned at my last job. This means that I am able to leave the legacy I want for the grandchildren. In addition to this, I am able to indulge in some luxuries I would never have bothered to think of, as well as being of help to several people in need. It has been of great satisfaction and delight to me to be able to help other people whenever I can.

I am still involved as an Elder in my church, and recently, I have been called upon to preach sermons every month. Amazingly, I found the skills that I have learned in the Sales Academy have helped to build my confidence in speaking from a platform. As many of the sessions at the Academy were on Zoom calls, we were broken into smaller groups, where everyone had a turn to practise speaking. We then had feedback from the rest of the group to help us improve our presentation. I can now look directly into people's faces as I speak in church and catch their attention. I have learnt to maintain a certain posture, as well as introduce changes in my tone of speech depending on what I am saying.

I run daily prayer sessions with members of the church, as well as lead a weekly Cell Group, which is a group of people who come together to pray and share thoughts on Scripture. These started during the time of my Elite Sales Boot Camp, and since then, I have learnt to turn up each day because, if there is one thing we were seriously encouraged to do by Nick Staab, it was to 'Turn up at all your sessions'!

I also now counsel certain members of the church who need a wise word to help them. At the back of my mind remains one of the most important statements that runs throughout the Academy, 'If you want results, then you are going to have to do things differently.' This has also been a turning point for many that I have spoken to.

I have been inspired to write by Nick Staab and Angela Wiafe, who is also a member of the Academy. They have both become best-selling authors on Amazon in the last couple of years! After listening to their amazing testimonies, I have been motivated to write. This was something that was in my heart for a long time, but I never did anything about it. Therefore, I took the plunge and began. I am proud to say that as I write this piece of work that you are now reading, I have finished the draft of my first book, which is a 90-day devotional on verses from The Bible! Having an accountability mentor encouraged me to set deadlines for my writing and to keep going until it was completed. It is now ready for editing. However, I have already started on my second book of Daily Devotions, as I now have set myself a goal to write four devotional books to cover one year. I have found that many of the principles in the Elite Sales Academy are very compatible with Biblical principles.

Writing the devotions has inspired me to write a chapter in this book, and even if I manage to encourage just one person to change their situation, then I would have achieved my goal. I cannot stop talking about the satisfaction that I have for these accomplishments, especially at my age. And there is still more to come, so I am considering writing the story of my life.

The fact that 'Sales' in this Academy is looked at as serving others makes me comfortable selling to people, as the goal is to help people buy something that makes them better for having it. The skills learnt in the Academy have taught me how best to help others decipher what they need to cause growth in their Christian walk and in their businesses. I have learnt to focus on Health, Wealth and Relationships, which relate to the principles I have also learnt from the Bible.

The Academy has taught me to set goals for myself in all areas of my life: personal goals, interpersonal goals, business goals, health and well-being goals, as well as financial goals. My life has been fuller and more meaningful as I tick off things I have accomplished, and I look forward to the next thing to do on my list. As much as this was done at the beginning of the year, I have learned to break them down into monthly and daily goals. We had an awesome session on the different ways to manage your time, and we got to realise that because we all had different personalities, the ways to manage time would be different for each of us!! We have also been taught to give ourselves a pat on the back every time we turn up at a mentoring session, and this has spilt over into being able to treat myself when I accomplish my goals. I look forward to my treats daily!

Not only have I learnt several skills which have added value to my life, but my lifestyle has changed. In the past, when I would get out of bed, it would take about an hour or more to get up and prepare for the day ahead properly. I had aches and pains, and many times, I would wake up with a headache. However, since the introduction of Performance sessions, things have changed for the better with my health and well-being.

My daily routine now includes exercise on a foldable treadmill at home. I set my time for thirty minutes and do my exercise while listening to Worship songs on my phone. I actually break out into a sweat when I do my routine!

I also now have a good hydration schedule! I have a two-litre water bottle, which I must complete by the end of the day. Plus, more if I finish it early!! Evidently, my lack of hydration was responsible for my daily headaches.

My sleep patterns have improved tremendously: from four hours of sleep a night now to five and a half to six hours a night.

Even my diet has changed! I was one of those who thought it was impossible at my age to change what I ate! I actually love my oats in the morning now! Fruits have become a large part of my diet, and I have found that I have a taste for exotic fruits! Has anyone tried lychees for dinner?

I have recently become a Mentor for the Academy in the area of Objection Handling! The one thing I have found out is that objections were made to be overcome. Everyone needs a push, gentle or hard, to take that step to get them to fulfil their in-built potential! There is absolutely nothing that cannot be overcome. If one person has done it, then you can, with the right attitude and encouragement! It has been an absolute thrill to be able to give back to Elite Sales Academy the things that have benefitted me.

My life has more meaning since I joined the Elite Sales Academy! I have met a number of awesome people! There is always someone to run things by who will give an honest opinion on your proposal. I have been motivated to become productive at this stage of my life, and I am well pleased with where I am and where I am going! When you are in the midst of motivated people, you cannot help but be motivated. My only regret is that this did not happen when I was much younger, BUT having said that, it is never too late for anyone to start!

My Top Tips:

Tip 1: If you do not make the most of your time, you lose it, never to get it back.

Tip 2: When you invest in yourself, you are motivated to make the best of your investment.

Tip 3: Why would you continue to do something that has not worked? It is time to make a change.

CHAPTER 9

The Power of Connection: A Relationship-Centric Approach to Selling

CELIA CONRAD

'We are in relationship to everybody and everything at all times. Whether we are aware of it or not, we are actually selling to each other every day. Being able to sell makes you more confident in yourself and positively impacts how you relate to the people in your life.'

- Celia Conrad

I AM A RELATIONSHIP expert. I am passionate about helping people create thriving and fulfilling relationships through positive transformative change. Whatever your relationship dilemma, whether personal or business-related, I can support you.

From healing heartbreak or personal loss, finding your ideal partner, and revamping your marriage to managing relationships in the workplace.

The two questions that I am often asked are why I chose to do this work and why I feel so passionate about it. To which my response is well, because of my own personal and professional experiences – more about my *why* below. The combination of the two has strengthened my desire to help others overcome relationship obstacles. My driving force is to make people's lives better.

But I haven't always worked as a relationship expert…

Before the start of the pandemic, I was engaged in a corporate role in the City on a bank remediation project. As well as being a Team Lead, part of my role was handling vulnerable clients' cases. This aspect of my role aligns very well with my previous extensive experience working as a specialist family lawyer. The position was challenging but also rewarding, and I enjoyed it. It is very edifying to be able to help people overcome problems and find solutions to situations which, on the face of it, may appear hopeless.

But in April 2020, a few weeks into Lockdown, my eldest brother was diagnosed with terminal cancer. With his diagnosis, the whole focus of my life shifted, and I gave up work to become his carer. When my brother died in February 2021, I was totally bereft. I felt as if my whole world had come crashing down. We were particularly close, and I struggled to accept his loss. I had already lost another elder brother and both my parents in tragic circumstances and had come out of a toxic relationship. It all seemed a complete waste and utterly meaningless. Where was the meaning in all of this?

I was unclear on the way forward, although I knew I did not want to return to the corporate world. But it sparked in me a heightened desire to help others struggling to heal from the pain of loss. This catalysed my decision to train as a Certified Grief Educator. This decision completely changed the trajectory of my life. It was intensely painful at times dealing with my own losses but also cathartic. I realised during the process that I had never fully grieved for the loss of my other brother or my parents. During the training, we dug deep into the various forms of personal loss, including divorce - the death of a marriage and a break-up - the death of a relationship. I remember thinking, 'Oh yes, I can definitely also help people struggling with relationship breakdown with my professional and personal experience. I can do this."

That was the incentive for me to train as an Accredited Break-Up and Divorce Coach Practitioner. I have subsequently become an Accredited Master Practitioner (specialising in domestic abuse) and obtained an ICF Accredited Relationship Coaching Diploma and a Level II IMM Certificate in Energy Healing. I am also a Mental Health First Aider MHFAider ®.

Fast forward to July 2022, I was completing my Relationship Coaching Diploma and wondering how best to extend my client base. I was searching online and came across a webinar on *YouTube* about how to generate some side income from property. I thought that was something I could consider while building my business, and I signed up for the online event the following weekend. The event was hosted by Nick Staab. I was not aware at that stage that Nick Staab was an Elite Sales Specialist, nor did I know that he was the founder of the Elite Sales Academy.

The Saturday arrived, and I eagerly logged on to listen to the first Masterclass on property, which was both interesting and informative. The second Masterclass was Nick's presentation on elite selling, and it is ironic when I look back at that day now, but I missed it. A friend called me with a relationship problem just when Nick started to speak, and I only caught the last few minutes of his presentation. I thought to myself, "Never mind. I hate sales anyway, so I'm really not bothered about missing that one." And dismissed it from my mind. I watched the third Masterclass on how to make a sustainable income from investing. I was actually going to log off at that point but decided to stay on for the final session of the day, the VIP session. This was also presented by Nick. When he started to talk about the importance of sales, I felt myself switching off. But then he made a statement which grabbed my attention, 'Selling is serving. And if we have a product or service which is genuinely the right fit for our customer or client, then it is actually a disservice not to sell it to them.'

That was a pivotal moment for me in my relationship with selling, the moment when my perspective on sales began to change.

I started to engage with Nick in the chat. I could see from the way he expressed himself that he was very passionate about sales. He was also very clear on his purpose - to educate as many people as possible on how to sell to serve. But then he mentioned the importance of having a tried and tested sales process completely built around serving the customer or client. He explained that he had created a 7-step process which could be tailored to any sales situation. And proceeded to elaborate on the steps and why his method was so effective. I was intrigued to learn more, which prompted me to sign up for his 3-day Elite Sales Bootcamp.

I realised that up until that point, I had never actually had a positive relationship with sales. But I also realised that this was because I was not at all comfortable with the whole mechanics of selling. It all seemed quite alien to me.

After all, selling comes with many negative connotations of 'snake oil' salesmen selling us products we neither want nor need and helping us part with our money, leaving us with buyer's remorse. The only person who is being served in those situations is the salesman serving himself.

Consequently, we have so many blocks around sales. We refer to people who are 'born salesmen' or who have 'the gift of the gab', but as with so many other things, it is actually a learned skill. With the right tools, practice and support, you can master the art of selling and become elite at it. An inability to sell comes down to mindset, lack of confidence, and not having a process to follow. More particularly, it is a process which deep dives into whether the 'sale' is of mutual benefit to all the parties concerned.

I have learned from Nick that when you use selling to serve, it is all about building rapport, connection, and trust. You must *only* ever sell to someone if the product or service is the right fit for them. As someone who is very much in favour of building relationships – it is the essence of what I do every day, after all, this resonates. This is the whole ethos of selling to serve.

Selling has relevance in the context of our day-to-day relationships. As I say in my quote at the beginning of this chapter, *'We are in relationship to everybody and everything at all times.'* Think about the time you persuaded your children to eat their greens. You were selling to them. Or a time when you persuaded a friend or a partner to change their arrangements to do something with you instead. You were selling to them. Persuasion is not the same as manipulation. Persuasion is when you open people's eyes to the benefits of doing something which is in their best interests. Manipulation is convincing someone to take a certain action which is not for the common good but only for the benefit of the manipulator.

When you are selling ethically, there is a fair exchange. And, if you are providing a service, then you are not being paid solely for your time with a client. You are also being paid for the value you bring to the client with the experience you have and your unique set of tools. It is a reciprocal relationship. This is the mindset and approach I adopt in my coaching practice. Requesting payment is a challenge I have had to work on in my business. This is a challenge that so many people in the giving professions have to overcome. And this is why an ethical way of selling is key to those of us who have a danger of over-giving.

Ethical selling enables me to reach more people. And, if I can help more people feel better through the services I provide as a relationship expert, enabling them to move forward from the pain of heartbreak and loss and build fulfilling and thriving relationships, then I have my purpose.

I mentioned earlier that I felt my own personal losses have no meaning. I have learned that meaning does not come from the loss. There can never be meaning in that. The meaning comes from within us. And for me, my meaning comes from my purpose to help as many people as I can who are struggling to heal from the pain of personal loss and for them to live as happy a life as possible.

I have found that there are actually three key issues people struggle with when it comes to healing matters of the heart: emotional overwhelm, feeling blocked from moving forward and not knowing how to change the status quo. I created my six-step H.E.A.L. I.T. Method ™ to address these key issues and enable my clients to break through the barriers keeping them stuck, empower them so that they can take back control, reclaim their lives and move forward with clarity and purpose.

That is what motivates me and inspires me. That is my vision. And being able to sell my services in an authentic way is part of that. When we are authentic in our message, we attract the right clients.

The reality is that life throws us curveballs all the time. There are things we can control, things we can influence and things over which we have no control. We cannot control the past, and we do not know what the future will bring. All we have is the present. How we respond to life events is what makes all the difference.

I feel privileged to do the work I do, and being able to reach as many people as possible and help them make that positive transformative change is an essential element of that.

And yes, it is far from easy dealing with all the knocks we receive on our life journey, but there is a way through, and I am living proof that with the right support, you can pick yourself up and move forward from pain and personal loss and reclaim your life.

When you learn to sell to serve, it has a huge impact on your confidence. How many of us lack self-worth or sell ourselves short? We are actually selling to ourselves every day. This means it is important we work on any limiting beliefs or negative thoughts we have about selling so we can give our best. There is a great deal of satisfaction to be gained from providing clients or customers with a service that changes the direction of their lives for the better and shows them how to take action, which will be of enormous benefit to them.

My top tips below are the basis of my ethos in life. I hope you will find them helpful.

I wish you success with your business. If I have helped you think about sales in a different way – and why it is vital to become elite at sales – by sharing my story, then all for the greater good.

My Top Tips:

Tip 1: Do what you love. Love what you do. Give great service and get paid well for it.

Tip 2: Always come from a place of authenticity. Your authentic self is the essence of who you are. It is your unique selling point (USP). You will attract the people who are the right fit for you and your business.

Tip 3: Life is a journey. Sometimes, we take a wrong turn, or life throws us curveballs. But more often than not, we can retrace our route and change direction. Learn from mistakes along the way and regard them as invaluable life experiences.

CHAPTER 10

What's Sales Got to Do with It: The Business We Are All In

DEA FILEVA

'If you can dream it, you can achieve it.'

- Zig Ziglar

I AM SITTING IN front of my switched-off TV in my beautiful Bayswater apartment in West Central London. I love the place; it's small but beautiful and serene, yet Hyde Park is just around the corner, and I run into a crowd of tourists as soon as I leave the building.

One may say I have everything: a great job with a recent astonishing salary increase, a nice little place in west London, a dream for many, and my own dream for a long time, too.

I am working in pre-sales; in fact, I am back at my old company selling corporate ERP software within the energy and fintech industry. After two years at Shell Trading as a business analyst, I moved back to my old company, this time in presales rather than consulting. Up until that point, I had worked for multiple multinationals and Fortune 500 companies, including Shell and PwC.

There is only one problem: I am drugged up to my eyeballs with antidepressants, stimulants, and the occasional muscle relaxant, lest I get an anxiety surge.

'There has to be another way', I think to myself. 'It can't be that I have to spend the rest of my life on these drugs just so I am able to work. And for what? To make money for corporations, not helping anyone directly.'

I had been diagnosed with adult ADHD and generalised anxiety disorder. In the past, I had also been diagnosed with mild depression. Shortly after that day, my friend came across someone who was not only a psychologist but worked with something called Emotional Freedom Technique. Hmm, it sounds all a bit *woo-woo*, but I decided to try it because I really trusted this practitioner.

We worked on a traumatic experience I had had as an adult and started tapping away (EFT is also called tapping, as one must tap on specific points, sort of like acupressure).

Oh my! In a few days, I felt like a new person. *It was like a weight had been lifted.*

Within a few days, I started remembering my past… my dreams, my passion, the fact that I have always wanted to be an entrepreneur, that I never actually wanted to work for anyone else, dreams that had been long buried and forgotten somewhere under the corporate ladder.

Right after my MSc in Economics, I had to get a job as I had huge student debts. Within just a few years, I managed to save up and pay them off. There was one problem, however. I had gone on a path which was divergent from my true self - not that there weren't some amazing perks about my corporate job, starting from international travel, hotel, and flight points, to feeling important as a high-flying consultant.

Unfortunately, the perks were just the surface; underneath, I had been losing myself. I found no meaning in the work I was doing; I wasn't helping anyone.

Little did I know back then how important it was for me to live a life centred around helping others. How could I? I barely knew myself. I just went from school to my degree to my first corporate job without giving it much thought. Following a prescribed path, wanting safety, financial stability, and the nice things that I didn't have so much of growing up, such as international travel. And I had managed to accumulate all these material things.

Until my pre-sales contract ended abruptly with no extension. I was too arrogant, they said. I think there was some personal(ity) conflict between my then boss and me, but regardless, the contract ended. It was the first time I had been kicked out of a job in a way. *Perhaps it is a sign?*

As I always did, I found a new job very quickly, this time working for a small start-up, reporting directly to my boss, and heading sales. Mind you, I had only been working in pre-sales before that, and I had years of consulting experience previously. What did I even know about sales? I guess I had gotten quite good at selling myself!

My boss and I didn't hit it off, I thought he was overly emotional, nosey, and did business quite the wrong way. One day, I left the office determined never to return. I quit there and then.

That all happened a few short months after the EFT therapy, and guess what? I think something had changed in me, and I could never go back to my previous self.

I remember my last day working at this start-up as if it were yesterday. My friends were visiting London, and we all went to a Coldplay concert. I couldn't focus on the concert, I couldn't focus on anything other than repeating to myself,

'I will never work for anyone ever again; I will be my own boss.'

Back then, I wasn't aware much of the power of the subconscious mind and the fact that it did not understand the negative. Say, 'I will never do this again', and your subconscious mind hears, 'I will do this again.' And I did work for other people during my entrepreneurial journey. However, this time, it was very different; it had a purpose, I did things that helped propel me in the right direction and learned things I needed to know in order to run my business. I never took up a corporate job again.

You know that moment in time when you make a decision, and you know your life is about to change?

You just don't know how yet, but you just know it will.

And so it did. A few months later, I started my first entrepreneurial activity: I wanted to build a website connecting therapists, coaches, and psychiatrists to clients. I wanted to use machine learning and my analytical mind to determine exactly which kind of therapy, modality, and person would suit what problem. I did have one teeny-tiny problem: despite my years in IT, I couldn't do the actual build myself, so I needed a Chief Technical Officer (CTO), and I couldn't find one.

So, I decided I would do it all on my own by hiring freelancers and contractors.

What a bad decision that turned out to be! I spent months searching, planning, trying to get some investor money, and bootstrapping my business. If you have ever worked for a start-up, you probably know that investors won't give you money unless you have a team.

Fast forward a year, and I was exhausted. But never mind being exhausted, I had also run out of literally all of my savings! My highly conditioned you-are-too-educated-for-this brain, however, wouldn't allow me to get just any job to make ends meet. At the same time, the well-paid contracting offers that recruiters used to shower me with a year before that, which I boldly rejected because, you know, 'I'm an entrepreneur now' had dried up!

What do I do? As you would, I started by having a proper panic attack. I didn't really quite know it was a panic attack back then. I was just walking down the street one day, and my heart started pounding. I thought I was going to die. The next thing I know, some people are helping me call 999, and I find myself at the A&E only to be told there was absolutely nothing wrong with me. Just take some rest.

Great. Rest is not what I need; food and shelter are. And what about my dream? Do I just quit and stop working on my start-up idea?

I wish I could say I have always been consistent. I wish I could say I never disappointed people. I wish, but it wouldn't be true. My friend, who was helping me with this project, never understood until years later why I suddenly stopped working on the start-up. Exhausted, scared, and hungry for safety again, I left it all and took up the first opportunity that was totally different and would earn me some money: working on a film set. For a few months, my life was magical, surrounded by colours, film stars and the magic of the seventh art. I made quite a hefty sum as well, as we worked from before dawn till after sunset for a few months in a roll. I even took an acting class, discovering a whole new part of me I knew I had somewhere inside, but which had also been put away in a 'stuff-other-people-do' box.

But a few months later, I realised there was a gap in me again. As much as I loved the world of performance and art (my mom is an artist, after all), I really, really missed business. Complicated personality, what can I say? I was and still am absolutely sure that one day, I would be able to combine the two.

***

You know when you make a wish, the universe responds with an opportunity?

It's up to you to take it up or not.

Out of nowhere, I got a text message inviting me to Jessen James' and James Nicholson's business event. The rest is history, as they say.

I started working as an event organiser, introducing some of the events as well as fulfilling my lifelong dream of being on stage! I also started assisting public speaking coaches who were offering courses to inspiring entrepreneurs. It was sort of like being on stage, even better, helping others get to that stage!

In 2020, I also published my first book. After I became a best-selling author, someone from the public speaking course I was helping at approached me to ask for help with their book and dream of being a published author.

There you go, another business opportunity: the money I made was very little, as the hours I actually spent working on it were countless. I hired an assistant, a designer, and a copywriter as well. I had to hire and fire ruthlessly at times, procrastinating at other times. Such a steep learning curve!

That was just before COVID-19 hit. One project wasn't enough, of course, to make ends meet, and other events had stopped, so after borrowing money to pay my rent from my partner a few times, he urged me to get a job.

I got a job in sales and customer services, lightyears below my qualifications.

'So what?', I thought.

I love the environment selling high-quality latex mattresses to high-end customers. Initially, people were still coming into the shop, and eventually, everything moved to phone service as the restrictions became more stringent. I had some financial stability, and at the same time, I was moving along with my business of book writing, putting out there more and more. Some more clients started coming in as writing a book was becoming more popular. Plus, as I often said in my marketing videos back then, you are stuck at home with all this time on your hands; when will there ever be a better time to write a book?

To date, I have worked with some of the most inspiring entrepreneurs, dentists, coaches, and therapists to help them publish their books from beginning to end! Every single one of them has become an Amazon Bestseller as well.

I met Nick Staab through the public speaking coaching I had done! What a cheerful, positive person Nick is. And as I was to find out later on, so hardworking and so unbelievably easy to work with, too.

I'm not quite sure what happened, but I am pretty sure that Nick sold *me* on helping him with his first book rather than the other way around! Talk about using sales in any situation!

Nick became a bestselling author in 2021 and broke any record I had had to date with any of my book coachees. He made it into the top 30 on Amazon!

It was a total blast! I couldn't be prouder of him.

Not only that, but I learnt so much from him and his book "Selling is Serving". I actually think it should be taught in schools.

Because what do we actually get taught in schools about real life, which sales is so much a part of? A subject for another day.

If you haven't got this book, and you are an entrepreneur, business owner, coach, therapist or… a human really, because sales is about *everything*, including how to get your kids to sleep or your partner to go to the theatre with you, then I highly recommend getting your copy.

You may be wondering, what does my story all have to do with sales?

Running a business and sales are inseparable. You see, running a business is nothing like most people imagine it to be. There are so many things you need to *unlearn*, and then so many new things you need to learn.

Running a business was not what I thought it would be at all: when I first quit my job, I thought, 'I got this, I have always been so hardworking and an A student; how hard can it be?'

Oh, how wrong I was! It is completely different. You have no schedule, no deadlines, no accountability, and no idea how to organise your day. Of course, you can put these things in place by having a team, business partners, accountability buddies, etc, but in my case, I had none of that initially.

So, a day would go by which I would have spent researching and reading and not actually moving the business forward. We all need structure and accountability. In fact, as counterintuitive as it may sound, you need structure in order to be able to create.

Not to mention, I realised despite the several jobs in presales and sales, I had no idea how to sell! Thank goodness for Nick, whom I learned and continue to learn so much from. I know I can always reach out to him when I have a question about a tough prospect or any sales situation I can't handle. I have genuinely never met a person who is always so positive and willing to help. And people say that sales is sleazy or salesy, but it does not have to be that way! Not if your heart is in what you do, if you are genuine and true to yourself and your clients.

At the end of 2020, I also signed up to study Rapid Transformational Therapy, a blend of hypnotherapy, psychotherapy and NLP run by the famous Marisa Peer. After becoming an RTT therapist, I also became an EFT practitioner and NLP practitioner.

Today, I am one of the best practitioners, helping people overcome emotional pain, bust money blocks, overcome limiting beliefs, heal their relationships, quit smoking, and assist in clearing many other issues as well. I also have a group of other inspiring practitioners whom I support by helping them write books and build websites. I am a therapist, a website designer, a book-writing coach.

And no, you do NOT need to choose one thing, as I have often been told along my journey. Not if you are talented in many things. If this is what you enjoy, having your fingers in multiple pies, then this is what you must do!

***

Selling is serving. Words of Nick and words I go by now, and I no longer fear "selling.", I know that I do incredible work for my clients. In the therapy profession, selling is most definitely serving, and if you focus on anything but that, then you are bound to have a dissonance in your belief system; as, on the one hand, you help and serve people, but on the other, you feel like you have to hard sell. But the truth is that you don't have to hard sell. You serve your clients from the moment they get on a discovery call with you. At the same time, you value your time, skills, and experience. I also no longer fear saying no to a client if it's not the right match. It would be a disservice to my other clients if I were to waste time on a client relationship which neither of us is ready for. So, staying true to yourself while having the inner confidence to know your worth is key.

My Top Tips:

Tip 1: Your environment matters more than anything in this life: just like the external environment - the people you surround yourself with, the things you watch, the things you hear on a daily basis, your internal environment matters too, what you eat, how much exercise, what you feel, the words and images you create in your head. All of that determines your very next step, and that step determines who you will be in the future.

Tip 2: You need to heal your past so you can build your future. Letting go of past trauma is no easy task, but it's a MUST if you want to be not just an achiever but also a VIP (a very inspired person).

Tip 3: Trust your intuition, your inner guidance, or whatever you may wish to call it: that little voice inside you that has no fear, no past and no future; it just knows what is right for you. If you can't hear it, then you need to revisit Tip #2 above.

CHAPTER 11

The Path to Success: A Heart-Led Journey

JESSICA NUTTER

'It is by going down into the abyss that we recover the treasures of life. Where you stumble, there lies your treasure.'

- Joseph Campbell

I AM A FULL-TIME Elite Sales Specialist serving various clients, I am also an appointed Mentor at the Elite Sales Academy, specialising in the area of helping clients to understand prospects' problems at an unconscious level.

Elite Sales brings a deep understanding of the unconscious mind and the programming that causes behaviour that often does not match with conscious goals and desired outcomes. My role as an Elite Sales Specialist is to help prospects overcome unconscious blocks during the sales process to help them make decisions that align with their conscious goals.

I also help others as a Certified Emotional Change Coach & Therapist, and Usui Reiki Master, supporting personal clients to overcome limiting beliefs, using NLP strategies, and completely transforming their energy frequency to make manifestation a reality.

I do what I do because many adults still have not created their desired outcome in life, whether that relates to health, wealth, or relationships, despite following logical strategies to achieve this, and I know I have the solution to free them from the shackles of fear and limiting beliefs!

The truth is our blocks to our desired reality are stored within our body. The body is the only vessel which brings messages from our unconscious to our conscious, and vice versa. The best way to harness unconscious programming is to train the unconscious through the body.

My work brings professional intervention of unconscious programming through working with the body and the energy field. The great thing is this work also weaves itself into Elite

Sales with the use of influencing positive body language and NLP simply with the art of conversation.

In this way, I help to completely transform people's life patterns to remove any blocks to their desired reality.

However, things weren't always this way. My old corporate job demanded long, unstructured hours, often working from 8 a.m. to 8 p.m. on various shift patterns. For many years, my life was a haze of colourful, yet dusty offices, cramped canteens, working so late I was overwhelmed with hunger - grabbing takeaways and catching buses! Most of my wage was disappearing on travel, office clothing, coffee, and convenience food! As a result, I felt drained, my health was suffering, and I had little energy to socialise or spend quality time with my family.

However, I worked alongside a variety of different colleagues and made some good friendships. I noticed I had a way of helping people, the way people with problems came to me to talk about it and each time left confirming that they felt a whole lot better than they had at the start of our conversation.

There were times that touched me, such as how the teams I worked with remembered my birthday and the time I was leaving one workplace, and the whole department clubbed together to put on a huge spread for me to say goodbye!

I was earning a wage however, I felt overlooked and unappreciated. No matter how hard I worked, I did not seem to be getting promoted at work despite my qualifications. And it seemed the harder I worked, the more unappreciated I felt! The irony I felt was that I was too good at my current job!

How did I reach such a situation?

Growing up, I only knew I had a strong desire to help people and enjoy my work through being creative.

I became a mum at 17, and from the outset, my main priority was providing for my children. As I realised just how expensive raising children is, I just wanted to earn a lot of money.

Six years later, I found myself at the age of 23. A younger sibling for my child and a separation had brought me to a new chapter. I had departed the town I had become accustomed to, leaving behind my part-time job and all the friends I had grown to know as part of my daily life.

A new set of circumstances was a challenge. However, I focused on getting my children into school and made some new friends in the local mums. During the day, I soon joined a local training centre to complete admin and business courses. I also found out about an evening class in law, which I decided to attend.

I loved being a mum; however, I believed that society did not value the importance of this contribution, particularly as a single young mum. I felt labelled as a failure. Compared to my old school friends who had just graduated from university, I also believed I did not have much hope to earn much money in the future.

Today, as a certified Emotional Change Coach and Therapist, I know these were simply limiting beliefs.

Limiting beliefs are simply an illusion and come from a place of fear. Fear is also an acronym for False Evidence Appearing Real.

Then, one sunny August day, I was informed that due to my recent certifications, I was qualified to start a law degree at the local college over the next three years.

After everything I had been through, I saw this opportunity to turn my life around!

There are many careers that a degree in law could lead to, and my only motivation was to make lots of money – ultimately to provide my children with as much support as I could for a secure financial future.

During my law degree, I went on a countryside break and met my husband-to-be, and as soon as I graduated, we got married and had two children over the next three years. By the time my youngest child was six months old, I wondered how I was going to continue with my legal studies and decided to complete my master's in law.

My career following this had massive highs and lows.

I moved into the area of business development and quickly discovered I had a natural talent for networking and engaging with people at all levels. I would describe my demeanour as bright and shiny with a magnetic personality that would draw leads to me. Whilst this was useful as a lead generator and brought huge revenue generation for my clients, what I lacked was a systematic strategy to close.

The moment to change came in 2020. I had generated a pipeline of high-ticket leads for a client when the pandemic struck!

My hot leads all had similar concerns about committing to any new decisions regarding their business, and I decided to pause my career to take a break!

At 39 years old, having worked full time alongside raising my four children with my husband, I also had other matters going on in my personal life! My dad had severe dementia, having been diagnosed shortly after my 30th birthday, and the last nine years had been spent being the main supporter for arranging my dad's care, visiting him, and supporting my extended family.

One of my most pleasing attributes is the ability to juggle several different projects at once, however, at this point, I truly felt drained and burnt out.

I decided to focus on home-schooling my 10 and 13 year olds and as I also have a desire to make the world a better place, and having the need for variety in life (which I was later to learn as an Elite Sales Specialist that this meant I fitted into a certain personality type which would be the director of all my life decisions) I also used this time to fulfil my wishes to become a temporary foster carer, taking in children for respite over the next year as the lockdown rules changed and children were allowed to move between homes.

Through this, I received specialist training about the lasting effects of trauma on the growing brain and the impact on overall health within the body, future decision making and belief patterns. This would support me with my later training in Emotional Change, NLP, and Elite Sales.

Meanwhile, I had time to reflect on my career.

At 39 years old, I had spent the last nine years trying to figure out how to build a profitable commission-based consultancy business, and with no formal training, I had gone from company to company, bringing in leads and marketing, yet never being the one to close the deal!

It had cost me time and money to meet business people for coffee in various places around the UK, and I felt what I lacked was a real sense of focus and authority. I was great at growing company revenue for others, yet I was struggling to keep my head above the water and pay my own bills. I decided enough was enough!

I had spent years learning from other entrepreneurs, but I knew the best people to learn from would be entrepreneurs who lived and breathed abundance and knew how to make serious money!

Determined to find the answer, my in-depth search led me to find high-level training in client acquisition taught by World Class Sales professionals. It was here that I realised the true nature of client acquisition, and it was a whole new level from my previous knowledge and skills gained in Business Development!

This is how I found myself in London on one of those mild Tuesdays in late November when the weather was dry, the sky was grey, and in the UK, it was now legal to open up business training events! I was on my way to my first day of my Professional Speak to Sell Bootcamp.

After a long journey through London, I finally opened the doors to the venue and breathed a huge sigh of relief! You know that feeling when you finally know you are in the correct place, right?

I knew I was an hour early and, upon arrival, found teas and coffees awaiting the attendees.

'I wonder if they need any support setting up?' I mused.

Just as I was wondering what to do next, I heard a strong male voice behind me.

'Good morning!'

I turned round … and there he stood!

Six feet tall, smart, suited and booted, athletically built and with a contagious brilliant white smile.

'Hi, I'm Nick!'

As a certified Usui Reiki Master and energy worker, I noticed I immediately felt drawn to his warm, yet grounded, energy.

We chatted for a few minutes whilst he registered my attendance, and I explained what had brought me to the bootcamp.

Shortly after this, I got to have a chat with the other organisers of the event: worldwide self-made multi-millionaire property investor, coach and mentor Liam Ryan and international business coach, mentor, and speaker Jessen James.

I was able to provide value by supporting and greeting other trainees as they arrived, building key relationships that were sure to bear fruits that I would in later years gain nourishment from, enabling me to provide even more value to the world and fulfil one of my core values: to make the world a better place.

What I noticed about this bootcamp was that Nick provided an astonishing amount of inspiration and support to me and others who attended.

Little did I know then that Nick was, over the next few years, about to become a major catalyst in my development journey.

It was over the next year, as I developed my sales strategy and professional presentation skills that I was taken on by the company Assets for Life as a high ticket closer and decided to join Nick's Elite Sales Academy to support my growing skills. I was surrounded by a completely different category of people who were entrepreneurial and positive.

Nick has been a fabulous mentor, and not only that, as I got to know him, I discovered he is a genuinely kind person with a huge heart of gold.

I have personally supported him to help thousands of people and be a catalyst in completely transforming the lives of those who want to make a success out of their lives and help others at the same time. This is what I love about working with him. In addition, working directly with him and surrounding myself with like-minded people through the Elite Sales Academy, Nick has genuinely helped me to completely transform my own life in every area.

With what I have learned from Nick's teaching about the primal functions of the human brain, I know - that we become a paragon of the five people we hang around with the most! This is why it is so important to surround ourselves with people who have succeeded in the area we wish to.

Today, my world could not be more different from where I started. I view my life as a journey, and the quality of it depends on the energetic frequency that I choose.

To do this, it is important to really embody Elite Sales and let it become a lifestyle.

This means taking care of myself in and out of work with the mindset of an athlete.

Athletes never stop working on themselves when they are not in the limelight performing! They constantly watch their diet, sleep, and watch what they absorb, working on their mindset as well as their body.

My life is a combination of travelling, spending precious time with my now four grown-up/teenage children, cherished friends, and my beloved dog. We love to spend time in some of the cities like London and Edinburgh and also retreat to the countryside in the Lake District.

Best of all, I am able to adequately serve others through selling!

Remember how I mentioned people would often come to me with problems and leave feeling better? As great a natural quality that was to have, without the strategy to sell, I was in no position to make any lasting difference to their lives. I could only offer temporary relief.

Now, I use selling as an effective tool to serve and bring people through limiting beliefs and fears that are blocking them so they can ultimately achieve their desired life-changing results!

Seeing the transformations appear right before my eyes with the thousands of clients helped through the Elite Sales Academy and seeing the ripple effect of this as these clients help others motivates me to do what I do. Having embodied Nick's strategies to the core, I know the only thing blocking people from achieving anything they want can be summed up to two things: 1. Lack of Elite Sales Education and 2. Limiting Beliefs.

These were the two biggest challenges in my life that I have personally overcome!

Today, I use the skills taught by Nick everywhere in life, whether I am working, negotiating for the best deal, or just encouraging my kids to eat their vegetables!

Most of all, I am able to sell to myself to make sure I am motivated to make the best choices! I have smashed my morning routine, overcome my sugar cravings, exercise regularly, and make sure I fill my life with abundance and joy! My health, wealth and relationships are better than I could have ever imagined, and this has extended my life expectancy and also my enjoyment of life overall.

My only regret is not knowing what I know now 20 years ago. Had I known this, I would have been wealthier and not have wasted time spent where my potential was limited. As a result, I would have been able to enjoy more quality time with my family and fill our lives with more meaningful memories.

However, we don't know what we don't know!

My vision for the future is to make up for lost time with my family and create amazing memories, teaching others how to do the same and step into wealth, health and happiness and completely break through any amount of fear!

My Top Tips:

Tip 1: Work from the inside out. Outer results will ultimately reflect our internal programming!

Tip 2: Identify the real issues your prospects face. Drill down and deal with these rather than the surface-level issues.

TIP 3: Review your outlook on problems. Remember, whatever you narrate to yourself, there are only ever two types of problems. Those that drain you, and those that motivate you. The good news is you always get to choose which type of problem you are faced with!

CHAPTER 12

Style Coaching: The Dual Face of Empowerment

LUCIA RESTANI

'Style, whether you embrace it or not, stands as the most influential and fast way to set the tone of any business and social interaction. Excel in this art, pave the way for success and fulfillment in life and career.'

\- Lucia Restani

My life's purpose is devoted to transforming and empowering as many women as possible through my holistic, personalised method that seamlessly blends style and coaching for an authentic and sustainable change.

In a world filled with preconceived notions and limiting beliefs, the journey of empowerment often begins with a change in perception. My mission is to challenge misconceptions and stereotypes, recognising the immense potential that thoughtful styling holds in empowering women to reach new heights both in their lives and in their careers. Style influences not only the wearer's thoughts and actions but also shapes others' perceptions, and especially in business, this is a potent asset to master.

Sadly, many underestimate the true impact of appearance, often fearing that looking good or seeking professional styling is superficial and not a sensible investment, ignoring how much our physiology (also through clothing) influences our cognitive mental processes and our emotions.

In the professional world, this apprehension is compounded by a stigma surrounding discussions of presence and dress code, limiting conversations, and discouraging feedback on the subject.

This misconception does a particular disservice to women, stifling their confidence and personal growth.

I will take you on a journey through my life, where destiny, passion, and a commitment to challenge societal norms led me to become a stylist and a coach dedicated to empowering women to embrace their full potential.

I believe that becoming a stylist was my destiny, perhaps due to my innate love for design, art, and any form of beauty, and also due to growing up in Italy, which is not only a country that displays beauty at every corner thanks to its architecture, landscape, and history, but is also the fashion capital of the world.

I was then nurtured by my mother, a skilled seamstress who instilled in me the value of quality over quantity and the significance of well-fitting clothing.

She always said, "You don't need too many clothes and even less, poor quality shoes. Best to have a few but quality pieces that fit well and can take you anywhere."

She is from an era where logos didn't exist; women had their clothes crafted from the best fabrics they could afford, and this is why they always looked immaculate. Surely, this is why my take on style is focused on the craftsmanship of the item rather than on the label it displays.

Besides, I was captivated by the meticulous attention and precision that goes into sartorial pieces, and the joy it brought to my mother's clients was undeniably rewarding to them.

This early exposure to the world of fashion and craftsmanship from a young age taught me to appreciate and value workmanship: how one's creative eye can truly transform a piece of cloth into a confident armour and not just a superficial layer.

It seems to have been a natural result that my innate gift and passion lie in unveiling the untapped potential within women, catalysing them to become true leaders in their private and professional lives.

This transformative journey unleashes a profound level of confidence and happiness, often exceeding expectations.

My journey was shaped further during my teens; I was one of the few girls involved in extracurricular journalism at a national level, where I was able to demonstrate a flair for presentation and the ability to inspire trust and professionalism. This was reflected in my frequent selection to present at conferences as well as to interview notable personalities such as authors and politicians and even raise funds for the school magazine and events.

It became evident that I had a distinctive perspective on how to present myself according to the scenario, and the people I was encountering united with the ability to communicate and to be taken seriously through both my appearance and my attitude. This was a great lesson to learn early on my path.

The turning point in my journey occurred during my final year of university studies in International Political Science. Listening to an interview on television with an Italian stylist in London was eye-opening. I felt a profound calling to follow a path that could positively impact women's lives. As she was describing her profession, I clearly remember thinking to myself: "This is me!". Without being fully aware of it, I was already styling friends and supporting their confidence growth.

Despite my limited English and no prior travel experience, I made the courageous decision to move to London in 2004 at 24, seeking invaluable experience in an international environment. Eventually, this journey took me across Europe, working with luxury brands in Paris and Milan.

A life-changing experience occurred in 2005 when I joined Wardrobe, a renowned consultancy boutique in Mayfair. Initially, the experience was rather intimidating. At the age of 25, with a decent command of English, I found myself among colleagues with impressive CVs. Who was I to influence and guide the style choices of some of the most influential women in the UK and the world? CEOs, entrepreneurs, MPs, and executives from major corporations entered the fitting room seeking my advice.

However, within a year, I not only overcame my initial apprehensions but also flourished. I had transformed into a stylist with a prestigious portfolio, becoming the top seller in the business.

Looking back, what has become crystal clear is that my motivation came from a genuine desire to alleviate the pressures faced by my clients. Witnessing their successes and newfound contentment and confidence in their appearance as women and professionals has been a deeply rewarding experience. Simultaneously, my innate selling skills have propelled my career forward, opening doors to new positions and increasing earnings within the company.

Unfortunately, even great things sometimes do end, and the consultancy boutique Wardrobe doesn't exist anymore. Still, I consider myself fortunate to have worked for that family-run business that not only allowed me to grow within a company, discovering and developing new skills as a visual merchandiser and fashion buyer, but also provided an invaluable opportunity. Without knowing it, I landed exactly where I was supposed to be. All the ingredients to shape my future were there: an international scenario filled with clients who were highly inspirational women and a wide offer of only made-in-Italy products of high quality crafted by family businesses.

Moreover, I will forever be grateful to the owner, Susie Faux, for enabling me to dive into a business mindset I had never been exposed to before as it wasn't part of my close environment and family culture, but that has enabled me to build my future.

After seven years, I decided to take a leap of faith and establish my consultancy, embarking on a journey that posed both personal challenges and a fresh perspective on sales. It became evident that while I had a great level of comfort when selling products, I encountered apprehension when promoting my services. This challenge was, in essence, a construct of my belief system. However, as I dedicated myself to personal growth, it became clear that investing in professional support was paramount.

This realisation, which took years to form fully, not only contributes to the growth of my business but also makes me a better coach. I firmly believe in practising what I preach and standing strong, exemplifying a thriving business that reflects the woman I have become. It serves as my living testimony that selling my services is the first step toward solving my clients' problems, with my sales being directly proportional to their increased level of confidence and achievements. I realise that I wouldn't be able to help as many women as I do today if I had not grown confident in the importance of genuine selling.

The same year after leaving my secure job and starting my solo journey figuring out how to build my consultancy from zero, a friend mentioned that the top luxury fashion brand women's showroom opened in London and as a new label in a city which historically never had the professional figure of Wholesale Seller, that could be an opportunity arising.

Let me first explain that at the time, it was quite an achievement to enter this glossy and exclusive field and usually, that happened mainly through personal recommendation. Moreover, they were generally not considering people from retail, as the misconception was that selling to buyers was a totally different game and more elevated service than selling to final customers in-store.

Also, what added an intriguing twist to this situation was that this friend failed the interview for the position; hence, her referral could have been completely ignored. With little to lose, I decided to pursue the opportunity should the manager show interest.

I don't want to sound pretentious, but as a matter of fact, I have never failed an interview so far, and I definitely didn't want to fail on this occasion. I am meticulous in getting ready for it, and what I wear is carefully studied to make sure it ticks the right boxes for the position I am applying for. Also, it needs to meet the interviewer's vision and leave a distinctive impression.

To put it into context, I will give you an example of this specific scenario.

As a brand, Tom Ford undoubtedly embodies glamour and sex appeal. However, upon conducting my research, I observed that the interviewer exuded a more minimal and classic style. Hence, I made a conscious choice to strike a balance with my outfit. I aimed to ensure that my attire not only respected the interviewer's preference but also conveyed my capability to align with the brand's vision.

We cannot avoid being judged; that is an instinct. Our subconscious connects visual cues to values and meanings, and this is what drives our economy. Thinking that we can avoid it or that it isn't important: well, think again.

In the meantime, as I was trying to develop my own business, a venture that I didn't realise posed a massive challenge. It not only required developing new skills but also placed tremendous pressure on enquiring who I was as a person; it was a new level of self-discovery.

Besides, I found myself on my own.

No one, apart from my partner at the time, truly understood my choice. Family, friends, and ex-colleagues were a bit shocked by me leaving a secure job where I had achieved success to start again with no guaranteed income while living in an expensive city like London. Yet, I felt I had to find a way to walk my own path.

The transition was rough, I must admit. I had no idea how to structure my day or how to lay the foundations of a successful profession. I had to find an accountant, and many new responsibilities emerged. Unexpectedly, I found that I was no longer the confident seller I used to be. The spotlight was now on me, not the product, and it presented a new set of challenges.

That's when I realised I needed to be among similar people, and more than anything, I needed guidance.

I have always been an action taker, sometimes even a little too hasty, so I signed up for the first big Business Marketing Program I was introduced to as I was eager to get unstuck. I was tired of walking in the fog, lacking clarity and somehow feeling misunderstood. That's how my coaching journey started and never ended, and in fact, today, I am part of this book thanks to my latest mentor, Nick Staab.

Investing in my self-development has helped me in shaping into the woman I am today. Without this, I may not have been able to express my skills fully and, most probably, establish my international consultancy.

Delving deep into my belief system has been quite a journey that has helped me to unveil many misconceptions we all absorb from culture, family, and social environment. It has been crucial in breaking free from self-sabotage.

The more I worked on myself, the better I became equipped to identify blockages my clients were facing and understand why, for some, embracing a change in their appearance was challenging.

At a glance, it seems quite straightforward. Basically, you just wear different clothes, you do your hair differently, you update your make-up, and so on.

However, that's not how it works.

Elevating one's presence means presenting oneself more authentically. It requires the strength to be who you choose to appear without hiding behind capabilities and roles.

This is why I have developed a method that now incorporates coaching.

In order to confidently transform into the best version that one can be, it's essential to understand where we limit ourselves, what we project into the world, and have a clear vision of who we want to become and how we want to act accordingly and how we wish to be perceived.

In my interactions with clients, a common source of frustration emerges when the anticipated promotion is delayed. Despite demonstrating their capabilities and ticking all the performance boxes, it appears insufficient. There's a sense of being held back, stuck in the current position, executing tasks with no change in attitude, and an ongoing expectation that recognition should have materialised by now.

Upon delving into their situation, I often discover that while their professional abilities shine, they haven't presented themselves as individuals ready to embrace the next level of leadership. I pose a straightforward question: 'Would you be comfortable featuring your face on a company marketing brochure right now?' If the answer is no, it becomes clear why advancement might face reservations from those in top positions. Even with a strong desire for progress, their actions may not align with the confidence and self-promotion needed for advancement.

Conversely, successful women at the pinnacle of their careers, having carefully curated their image, grapple with a dilemma. Long cast in a specific mould, they find it challenging to appear more approachable, adaptable, or in alignment with their femininity without compromising the authority aura required for their position. The struggle lies in incorporating a higher level of self-expression into their appearance, particularly after achieving significant wealth and freedom.

While there's no one-size-fits-all formula, the key lies in fostering self-awareness and partnering with an objective professional for a natural transformation. It's akin to working with a personal trainer – initially challenging but immensely motivating, pushing one to raise the bar with each session, ultimately yielding visible results.

Witnessing and celebrating the personal and professional successes of my clients brings immense satisfaction. It fuels my passion, propelling me to constantly evaluate how I can enhance my approach and support more women.

I am grateful each time a client takes the courageous leap to embark on this transformative journey with me. The privilege of being welcomed into their intimate sphere, both emotionally and physically, is never taken for granted. I understand it requires courage and a leap of faith, as I commit to delivering results that are challenging to describe but have a practical and visionary impact.

Admittedly, there have been moments when I contemplated the allure of a straightforward career path. I possess the skills and intelligence to excel in such a trajectory. However, the immeasurable value lies in witnessing the sheer joy in my clients' eyes as they gaze into the mirror and exclaim, 'I never thought it possible to look like this.' The immense satisfaction of cheering on their success, especially when that long-awaited promotion or new opportunity materialises, is truly gratifying.

Moreover, there's a unique sense of fulfilment in ensuring that, during their celebratory moments with family, I've alleviated any attire-related stress. My goal is to let them fully immerse themselves in creating unforgettable memories, unburdened by style concerns.

Looking ahead, my vision is to advocate the idea that women should never feel burdened by guilt or pressure when it comes to tending to their presence. Openly discussing the reliance on professional support, be it in coaching or styling, should not be a concealed aspect of our journey. Instead, it should stand as proof of our commitment to personal evolution and leadership growth.

In fostering genuine sisterhood, there should be comfort in providing honest feedback that has the power to open someone's eyes. Equally important is the willingness to share personal experiences to empower others. It is within this open dialogue that true empowerment and support thrive.

I sincerely hope that this chapter will sow seeds of contemplation and, perhaps, serve as inspiration for individuals of any gender to explore the notion of whether there's something more or different they can do to thrive and embrace life to the fullest.

A heartfelt thank you to Nick for providing me with the opportunity to share my voice.

My Top Tips:

Tip 1: Embrace Your Future Now. Delaying the appearance of your desired role until you attain it is a futile strategy. The truth is, it might never materialise. Take charge of the person you aspire to be. Act and present yourself as the leader you envision. Opting for the safe route is seldom rewarding; to ascend, you must radiate and shine.

Tip 2: Shop Less - Shop Smarter. Cultivate a list of wardrobe essentials and allocate your resources wisely on each item. While it may require scaling back on shopping initially, taking a few seasons to curate a purposeful wardrobe ensures longevity and better service to your style needs.

Tip 3: Invest in Your Growth. Learn from those who surpass your achievements. Embrace the opportunity to collaborate with professionals who specialise in enhancing your presence. Accelerate your journey toward your goals with greater ease by being open to external insights. Objectivity about oneself can be challenging; a professional brings a detached perspective that fosters valuable insights.

CHAPTER 13

Thriving Through Trials: Embracing Life's Brighter Path

MATTHEW JEFFERY

'You could be good today. But instead, you choose tomorrow.'

- Marcus Aurelius,
the Last Roman Emperor of
The Golden Age of Rome

Tomorrow is a familiar word, but do we genuinely give it the importance it deserves?

I am profoundly privileged to hold the role of Expert Speaker in Fulfilment and Motivation.

Engaging and enriching people's lives is a rewarding pursuit in many ways.

It is also humbling, serving as a counterbalance to the relentless pressures of modern-day life. Too often, we become trapped in the day-to-day grind, losing sight of fleeting moments. These are moments we could be savouring, moments that could, in turn, nourish our mental and physical well-being.

Like many others, I once took tomorrow for granted as an assumed concept, a given.

I was entrenched in a high-profile, demanding career, entrusted with multi-million-pound projects that promised societal well-being for current and future generations and commercial prosperity. This was something I was genuinely passionate about and enjoyed.

But in January 2022, the veneer of assumption was shattered when I bore witness to my father's passing. The loss of a loved one is never a simple ordeal. Though inevitable, we can never truly prepare for the loss of a parent. I had little time to brace myself as his health declined rapidly over two weeks during one of the Covid lockdowns. This meant visiting the hospital, and then hospice was highly restricted and limited to an hour a day for two pre-arranged visitors. Sometimes, even that was not possible.

The emotional impact on myself and the family was akin to a sledgehammer strike.

The fateful call came just as I had concluded a presentation before a senior-level investment group, unveiling a three-million-pound investment project that would lead the way for future projects and one which had consumed the preceding two years of my life.

This project bore a poignant connection to my father; it was one of the last topics we discussed while he still could converse. It was also one of the occasions he articulated his pride in me. Our relationship had previously faced challenges, yet it was unyielding, but my father hailed from a generation that grappled with expressing emotions. I stood by his side as he faded away during my daily visits to the hospital and hospice - a gruelling two weeks.

On January 31st, 2022, I delivered my father's eulogy and watched as his casket was tenderly lowered into the earth. 'Sleep now, Dad' were the words that came to me.

Four weeks later, I suffered a seizure and collapsed on my kitchen floor, enduring a heart attack followed by two cardiac arrests. I traversed the threshold of death itself. My world plunged into utter darkness. I was dead.

As I was resuscitated, a surreal semi-consciousness enveloped me. I remember the absolute void of blackness and a bone-chilling cold. I contemplated my demise and wondered if I would be reunited with my father. I experienced an eerie sensation of existence devoid of physical form. Then, unfamiliar voices reached me.

'I must be dead,' I thought.

Although my heart had restarted, I was blind. I had no sense of my own body or if I was actually alive or dead. Suddenly, the cold abyss dissipated as my sight was restored. The first image to meet my gaze was that of a paramedic urging me to keep fighting. So, I did.

I may have another tomorrow after all.

With odds of survival as low as 7%, the medical team told me I had endured two of the most fatal cardiac events imaginable. It was bewildering and terrifying. Despite maintaining a lifestyle of health, fitness, and athleticism, my body had been betraying me for months, and I was diagnosed with chronic fatigue syndrome to explain my ongoing condition. Little did anyone know what the root cause actually was. That clarity came later, for my health had started to deteriorate following a vaccination.

Blood clots had formed in one of my arteries to such an extent that the cardiologist and his team almost had to give up on clearing them as I lay medicated but conscious in the operating theatre.

They were baffled by why I was in front of them - it didn't make sense, given my fitness and active lifestyle.

All of us fought on clinging to the remaining thin threads of life, and after some hours, way beyond the expectation of time for such an invasive procedure, I was taken out of the operating theatre and placed into the Cardiac Critical Care Unit.

I was exhausted and confused. Sleep did not come easily, if at all.

During this tumultuous period, my marriage unravelled.

Some months before the cardiac events, my partner of fourteen years had embarked on a relationship with another man. The explanation was that 'I was enough', yet how could that be if she desired another? I felt bewildered, wounded and unlovable.

Friendships began to shift and dissolve. Lines were being drawn in advance. I didn't fully see it at the time until later on. Ignorance can be bliss sometimes, and the truth does not always fit desired agendas and narratives. I immersed myself in work to distract and cope, straying from my instincts in a misguided attempt to salvage the marriage by giving her what she wanted.

Little did I know, my vision had already been clouded long before my cardiac ordeals temporarily took it away.

I was sad, at times angry, and adrift. Few knew of our situation.

I was regularly told, 'We control the narrative.'

Yet I felt like I had no control.

It was a time of loneliness.

I acquiesced to the notion of an 'open marriage', although it bore little resemblance to such. My partner desired her new suitor exclusively. It had never been on our radar within our marriage before, and I hesitated to fully engage in this so-called modern way forward. I soon knew I did not want to pursue this lifestyle change for myself in the way my partner had. My experiences via the online scene were hollow and misleading. It may have seemed like it could be 'fun' initially, but that was just an illusion. In truth, it did more harm than good. I felt foolish, and I could see the frustration in my partner because I was not engaging in physical relations with another while she was. Our relationship took another turn as the distance grew.

I longed for what we had envisioned and discussed before she met him and others who endorsed such lifestyles - or so I believed.

Our situation was not for public discussion with family or friends. The few that did know were carefully selected and managed. I felt like a lesser man for allowing such manipulation. At the time, I thought I was doing the right thing, doing what I believed could salvage the marriage and protect her and us.

I should have been wiser to the fact there was no 'us', and there hadn't been for months.

I allowed an idea to overtake reality. With it, the hurt was less, or so I thought. The truth was it was just delayed.

I had ceased to be myself.

I felt more alone, even within the confines of a marriage that had dwindled into a hurtful solitude. My partner spent little time at our shared abode; when she was present, we occupied separate corners of the house. Our routine of cooking and dining together, once an intimate bonding ritual, had grown cold and distant.

The night of my cardiac crisis, she returned home fifteen minutes prior, having been away all weekend.

I was told later such cardiac events often come with an emotional trigger. If I think about it, I can still recall the strange sensation of physical pain of the heart attack that was the precursor to the cardiac arrest.

I am grateful for her efforts to save my heart and life that night. I recognise the trauma it entailed for her and the act of one human helping another despite our relationship breakdown.

Upon my hospital discharge, I could scarcely stand, let alone walk. I was trapped in physical and emotional agony of an unprecedented magnitude. My body and mind were shattered beyond anything I had ever endured. I embarked on cardiac recovery, making commendable progress, yet the road ahead remained long and arduous.

I will also remain grateful for the moment she broke my heart after having helped save it. Merely eight days after my release from the hospital, she departed to be with her new partner for a long weekend, and four weeks later, she declared her intent for divorce, instructing me that I would have to vacate our home.

At 49 years of age, my world had been upended.

I teetered on the precipice of despair, engaging with my cardiac support nurse in a conversation centred on 'suicide watch'. It was a pivotal juncture, a choice—a simple one. I had to decide between the desire to persist or surrender. I chose to stay. And thus, I began my new life, which has overtaken my previous one in many positive ways.

Four months after experiencing clinical death, I achieved the most remarkable cardiac recovery results, astonishing the cardiac nursing staff. I was invited to speak to other cardiac survivors, offering motivation.

Another four months later, I found myself hiking through American National Parks, exploring cave systems in Kentucky, experiencing the varied and lively Nashville music scene, and traversing the urban sprawl of Chicago.

I was alive and brimming with newfound life.

As part of my recovery journey, I delved into self-development courses and encountered the provider Assets for Life. Amidst my deliberations, I gravitated toward them as my top choice.

Here, I crossed paths with Nick Staab, and my life took a dramatic turn.

Mentorship and deep self-development had never figured prominently on my radar. This uncharted territory was refreshing and full of promise. I wholeheartedly embraced it.

My perspective underwent a seismic shift, leading to a substantial enhancement in my quality of life. Understanding sales as a service and solution provision reshaped my world, impacting personal relationships, professional endeavours, and every facet in between. While I had always been service-oriented and people-centric, this journey took me to deeper realms.

I was surrounded by remarkable individuals who uplifted and supported one another, eschewing the toxic rivalries of previous social circles. I cut away detrimental relationships, opting for positivity aligning with my values. My positivity and self-worth surged.

With unwavering clarity, I grasped the 'Rule of Five'—the idea that we become the average of the five people we most closely associate with. The phrase 'actions speak louder than words' had never been so clearly demonstrated as it was at this time. Clearly, the truth didn't fit the agendas of others, as demonstrated by the behaviours of some. Immature social interactions and dramas that once trapped me dissipated, and while temptation beckoned, I charted a nobler course of non-participation with former so-called friendships, moving on and away. I chose to let my actions show my strength of will without the need for words or re-engaging with situations that were clearly not what they could or should have been.

This newfound understanding was akin to the sudden light when my sight returned, seeing the paramedic bidding me to 'Keep fighting, Matthew!'

My transformation was driven by the wisdom gained through mentorship and the concept of sales as a service. To understand a problem thoroughly and then be able to offer a solution. Far from the usual labels attached to sales skills.

My journey has been nothing short of extraordinary, an odyssey as profound as any human life can encompass. Yet, I am acutely aware that others bear their tales of trials and triumphs. I do not claim exceptionality but rather acknowledge my good fortune in having a story that impacts others profoundly positively. I possess the gift of tomorrow, but I am resolute in my commitment not to squander the precious moments of today.

Today, I am surrounded by remarkable individuals with whom I work closely.

Through the reciprocal exchange of mentorship, I am guided by world-class figures: Nick Staab, Liam Ryan, Adam Stott, Phil Elder, and the legendary Jim Francis. They are not merely mentors in my professional journey; they are among my dearest friends on this transformative path. I hold deep respect and affection for them all.

I am also blessed to belong to a robust and supportive community. I previously spoke of the importance of finding like-minded individuals, and I have found my tribe. We each harbour ambitions and dreams, bound by a shared desire to witness one another achieve fulfilment and success in these pursuits.

My retreat companion and confidant, Ruth, will forever remain close no matter where we find ourselves. Our shared experience of navigating complete breakdowns and subsequent rebuilding represents one of the most profound chapters of my life. It is a chapter that belongs to us, an irreplaceable moment in time and space.

And with these experiences have come other friendships on a far more elevated level of bonding and adulthood. I value each one of them.

Now, let me share an uncomfortable truth: We are all, in essence, salespeople.

I know that may seem blunt, but it is true.

The act of selling permeates every aspect of our lives. It is merely a matter of shifting our perspective and redefining what 'selling' signifies. In doing so, we can recognise it as a service to ourselves and those around us.

As a Professional Speaker and Mentor, I wholeheartedly embrace selling as a service. Through this lens, I connect deeply with my audience and clients, delving into their struggles to unearth solutions that yield tangible improvements in their lives and the lives of those they touch. This approach is a force for good, empowering, and heart-warming to witness.

I have used sales skills to improve my career prospects as I grow my speaking career. It has helped me to achieve six figures in income. This has been nothing short of game changing.

When people inquire about my motivation for what I do, I offer this simple answer:

It is not selfish to aspire to the best that life can offer. Our prerogative is to seek and savour the finest experiences life can provide. Everyone defines their version of this ideal, and by collaborating with others, they can manifest it, whatever form it may take.

For those who doubt their ability to overcome obstacles, I implore you to pause and consider all that you have already achieved in your life and all that remains on your journey. Your desires and aspirations are the fuel that propels you forward.

Throughout my journey, I have confronted the monumental challenges of divorce, death, and displacement. Yet, despite these towering trials, I continue to look optimistic. I focus on today, savouring its richness, and in doing so, I lay the foundation for a brighter tomorrow.

One challenge I presently confront is expanding the reach of my speaking engagements, for I am fervently driven to touch more lives and effect positive change. I wish to convey to others that they are not alone, that they are not unloved or unlovable, and that they stand far from the end of their journey. They are, in fact, good today.

We are presented with choices in life, and today's choices shape tomorrow's realities. It is a reminder that tomorrow is not guaranteed, urging us to seize the opportunities of today.

Selling is not the selling of years gone by. It is a service and solution provision from one human to another. People do business with people, so when you understand the importance of selling and sales, you understand yourself and others.

If I, in the face of adversity and profound challenges, can find the strength to persevere and prosper, so too can you.

Embrace your inner Fulfilled Warrior today and watch your tomorrow unfold brighter than you ever imagined. Trust me on this. It is waiting for you today, not tomorrow, but today.

My Top Tips:

Tip 1: Seek out mentors and craft your unique plan.

Tip 2: Do not listen to 'noise' and have faith in yourself.

Tip 3: Initiate decisive action and follow it, and you will be successful.

CHAPTER 14

The Hidden Power of Introversion: Finding Your Voice

ANGELA WOOD

'Shyness is not a weakness, but a gentle strength that allows you to observe the world with a unique perspective and heightened sense of awareness.'

- Angela Wood

S*HYNESS (FOR TEENS)* | *Nemours KidsHealth* defines shyness as 'an emotion that affects how a person feels and behaves around others. Shyness can mean feeling uncomfortable, self-conscious, nervous, bashful, timid, or insecure.' People who feel shy sometimes notice physical sensations like blushing or feeling speechless, shaky, or breathless, which can, at times, be very debilitating in social situations, depending on the severity of the reaction.

I have included this definition as, for some lucky people who have never experienced the feeling of shyness, it can be a difficult concept to understand. It is not something that can be just 'snapped out of' and takes a great deal of consistent effort to overcome.

***

I am shy! I have always been shy.

Or have I?

Babies are not born shy, so is it nature or nurture?

Some of my earliest memories include times when the family went to visit friends, and I remember my mum introducing me with the words, 'This is Angela. She's shy.'

So, was I shy, or was I simply doing as I was told?

There is evidence to suggest that some individuals may have a genetic predisposition towards introversion, which can influence a person's temperament, making them more prone to shyness in social settings, but genetics alone do not determine shyness.

Early childhood experiences and upbringing can significantly shape an individual's behaviour and self-perception. Parental labels and early interactions with family and friends, especially in the formative years, can have a massive impact on how we view ourselves. The things that a child is told when young and the labels that they have put on them can become a self-fulfilling prophecy.

Therefore, shyness itself is a complex interplay between genetic predisposition and early experiences.

So, whatever the reason, this state of 'shyness' stayed with me throughout my childhood, teens, and early adulthood, and I had a severe lack of confidence. There were many situations where I would hardly speak, frozen in fear. I would feel nervous and self-conscious in social situations (and, truth be told, on some occasions, I still do).

I basically had no voice and was often accused of being 'stuck up' and 'stand-offish' and, laughably, even 'posh'. So, when, at age 16, my mum forced me to apply for a Saturday job at a shop called Rumbelows, where I had to sell electrical appliances to the public, and it was my worst nightmare.

Somehow, I don't know how I actually got the job, but I have to be honest, I was rubbish at selling anything. I would get incredibly nervous when talking to customers and 'trying to convince them' that they should buy a certain product. I was much better behind the scenes doing the admin side of the job - raising invoices, placing orders, and cashing up the till.

In a world that often celebrates extroversion and assertiveness, shyness can often be seen as a weakness or a hindrance. Still, the thing was, I had never had any actual training in how to sell, how to speak to people in a sales environment, or how to overcome objections. The only training that I had received for this job was how to change a plug and fill in an order form.

The lack of training and proper guidance in sales and interpersonal skills only exacerbated my nervousness, lack of confidence and shyness. This experience sent me down a route of trying to avoid being 'in sales', so I decided to go to catering college.

This decision, as an alternative to sales, seemed like a plausible one. After all, surely working in a restaurant or hotel meant I didn't have to sell anything, right?

Hahaha! How wrong I was. I quickly discovered that working in the hospitality industry also demands persuasive interpersonal skills.

Selling the specials on the menu when the customer really just wanted the classics.

Selling the upgrade hotel rooms when the customer really wanted to pay for the basic.

Selling the 'Cocktail of the Week' when the customer really just wanted a beer.

The list was endless.

While initially, it may have seemed a misguided choice to enter this industry to escape from sales, it presented me with the opportunity to start confronting my shyness and finding my voice. I enjoyed interacting with some of the customers and became more comfortable engaging with people. Even if I still wasn't any good at sales, my confidence started to grow a little.

My problem was that I always had the mindset that I had to try and convince people, against their will, that they needed to buy more or spend more. I now realise that this mindset was the real hindrance in my sales journey rather than my shyness.

The jury is still out on that one, by the way, as I no longer truly believe that I am 'shy'.

Many people who are 'shy' are deep-thinking and analytical, are active listeners and have deep empathy. They can be very focused and pay attention to detail. They are good planners and indulge in thoughtful communication. A 'shy' person has a unique set of talents that can be harnessed as strengths.

The catering part of my journey lasted several years into my early adulthood. Although my confidence had grown, I found that I didn't really feel passionate about being in hospitality. What I was passionate about was the human body. Biology had always been a favourite subject at school, and over the years, I had found a lot of interest in reading books about massage, reflexology, and anatomy. How the mind-body connection works was fascinating.

So, after having my third child, I took the plunge and trained as a massage therapist. Quickly following the basic massage qualification with sports massage and continuing with several other massage modalities. I loved it and thought,

'This is going to be great. I'll be able to help people by doing something I love while earning lots of money!'

There was just one drawback. Where would I find my customers?

I realised that I had to start selling again, but this time, I had to sell ME, which I found more difficult.

Yes, I had a service but no actual physical product and in order for people to want my service, I had to sell them the idea that I was the best person to provide that service. How on earth was I going to do that?

As it turned out, I was lucky enough to have a family friend who booked a treatment and became my first paying customer, who then went on to recommend me to a few other people, which was great but wasn't enough to earn a living. I tried many different ways of advertising; some of them were scams, and some were ineffective, and I lost more money than I gained. However, despite the setbacks, challenges, and financial losses, I refused to give up on my dream of being a successful therapist and continued to explore different ways to promote my services. Eventually, my determination and tenacity started to pay off, and I started to build a nice client base. Although it was small, I was happy. I had a business that was bringing in a sufficient income, not huge but sufficient, and I could work around my family commitments. My hours of work were flexible and at my discretion, so I could still attend school events and take my children to their clubs, such as football and scouts. I thought that I was living the dream.

However, when my marriage ended, I realised I needed to up my game. I was now a single mum of four and the main breadwinner. It was time to learn how to sell myself properly.

At this point, I had been working as a therapist for around ten years, so I took an opportunity offered to me to teach massage workshops to other therapists, teaching them various different massage modalities. This took me right out of my comfort zone, as rather than speaking to individuals on a one-to-one basis, I was now standing at the front of a classroom, sharing my knowledge with a whole room full of people.

The interview phase entailed conducting a class in the presence of a supervisor, which presented a significant challenge for me. I found myself under scrutiny for every aspect of my performance, from my words and demeanour to my interactions with the students. Thankfully, my resilience, determination and drawing on my past experiences got me through the interview, and I continued to teach for a further five years alongside running my mobile massage practice.

Transitioning from a massage therapist to an educator marked a significant turning point in my career and confidence. However, in 2020, the onset of the COVID pandemic brought about a major setback and a new set of challenges. I had already ceased teaching, and now, with the event of lockdowns, I could no longer provide in-person treatments. Emerging from the lockdowns, it became evident the world had changed. The conventional marketing and selling strategies that once served me were no longer effective, necessitating the need for a new approach to rebuild my business.

It was during this period of regrowth that I discovered The Elite Sales Academy, and it dawned on me that even after all these years, I was still operating with the same mindset that had shaped my approach to sales and selling back when I was working in Rumbelows and the hospitality industry.

I was approaching my marketing from a place of having to convince people to buy my services rather than from a place of providing a service that they desperately needed.

After twenty years as a therapist, it felt as if I were embarking on a fresh start with my business and starting from scratch. For years, I had relied on the traditional marketing methods that had served me well, but I had come to realise that it was a mediocre approach and had resulted in a relatively small client base. If I truly desired to build a thriving business, it was clear that I needed to make a significant shift in mindset. If I really wanted to have a successful business, I was going to need to embrace the lessons from my past failures and push myself even further out of my comfort zone.

The fact is, however, that this leap out of my comfort zone was the most fun and thrilling adventure ever.

So, with the help and guidance of the coaches and mentors of the Elite Sales Academy, Assets for Life and Big Business Events, I have learnt how to have meaningful conversations that help me to serve others to the best of my ability without the need to 'force' a sale. I have learnt how to overcome objections easily, even before they arise so that the potential client actually feels at ease saying 'YES' to whatever service I am currently promoting. I have learnt to feel comfortable in my own skin, and shyness is no longer a stumbling block. In fact, I now see it as a strength, as this particular trait of my personality means that I have the ability to listen deeply and empathise with the person that I am interacting with.

The mindset that I now have is that the services I offer have a real benefit to somebody, so why should I deprive that person of my service by not shouting about it? I no longer have to convince anybody to buy my services. All I need to be doing is having more conversations with people. Find out about them. What are their concerns, their problems, their desires, and how can my service help with these?

What I have learnt through my experiences is that sales or selling in one form or another isn't just a career. Sales is a part of every aspect of your life every single day. It is part of more jobs than you can imagine, even if they don't have the word sales in the title. It is part of all of your relationships with your family, friends and everyone that you interact with. Everyone that you engage with is building a perception of you, and the truth is that these perceptions can be influenced by using your sales skills.

My journey from becoming a massage therapist to establishing myself as a successful entrepreneur has taken resilience and determination. It has not just been about mastering massage techniques but also learning how to promote myself and my services effectively.

There have been many challenges along the way. Still, I have realised many of these challenges have been the result of a lack of knowledge and training, particularly around sales and marketing.

There was no time during any of my massage training that I learnt how to market and promote my business effectively or how to obtain my first paying client, but I have had the honour to have found mentors who can guide and advise me on these details and teach me the skills.

I have now cultivated a deep passion for mentoring and empowering the new generation of massage therapists, equipping them with the tools that they need to kickstart, expand and flourish in their own massage practices. With two decades of expertise under my belt, I've harnessed my knowledge, honed my skills, and leveraged my extensive experiences to develop a comprehensive training and mentorship programme. Not only does this programme impart essential massage qualifications, but it also fast-tracks the path to success, serving as a roadmap to help newcomers to the industry navigate their journey.

I have walked the path and learnt from my own mistakes so that others can avoid the pitfalls and thrive in their careers.

My Top Tips:

Tip 1: It is important to remember that shyness, introversion, or lack of confidence are not permanent traits. They can be developed and improved over time with practice. If you want to overcome shyness or build self-confidence, seek out opportunities for personal growth and professional development. Begin by putting yourself in low-pressure social situations where you feel comfortable and set small, achievable goals for yourself. For example, aim to initiate a conversation with one new person at a social event or make eye contact and smile at a stranger.

Tip 2: If you have a fear of selling or believe that it is something you are unable to do, shift your mindset and focus on building a relationship instead of solely focusing on making a sale. Approach each interaction as an opportunity to connect with someone, understand their needs and provide value. By genuinely listening and showing an interest in their needs, desires and wants, you can build trust and can serve them with your product or service rather than sell to them.

Tip 3: Becoming an expert in sales of any kind is a journey that involves stepping out of your comfort zone and embracing new challenges. This may feel scary and uncomfortable, but it will ultimately lead to greater self-confidence and the life that you dream of. Your comfort zone is a nice and safe place, but outside your comfort zone is where the magic happens.

CHAPTER 15

Create Your Own Future - It Is Your Choice...

DIANE SIMPSON

'Watch your thoughts. They become your words.
Watch your words. They become your actions.
Watch your actions. They become your character.
Watch your character. It becomes your destiny...'

- Lau Tzu

IN THAT QUOTE from Lau Tzu, the famous ancient philosopher, lies the secret to true manifestation.

It says that we don't manifest what we want but what we are.

If you want love, become a loving person.

If you want to receive abundance, become a generous giver.

If you want respect, respect others.

If you want success, embrace challenges.

So remember, the secret to manifestation is in your transformation.

Focus on becoming, not just desiring.

My Personal Quote of my Life....

You have your Dreams...

You have your Mindset...

Move forward with Positivity...

And accomplish your Goals...

Create your Future!

Nobody else will do it for you.

Life should be Fun...

- Diane Simpson

So...This is what we do...

Lose Yourself / Discover Yourself

Yellowtop Country Park and Still Rabbit Lodges

Your ultimate romantic break and family getaway

Situated on the outskirts of historic York at the foot of the Yorkshire Wolds

Make the time to reconnect with people that are important in your life
Create lasting memories with your family or that special someone
Individually themed lodges, excellent carp fishing on-site
Nature and wildlife on your doorstep
Relax - after all, you deserve it
Lose yourself / discover yourself

This is our aim, our branding and our elevator pitch in one short burst.

The creation of Yellowtop Country Park commenced twenty years ago. The site on which we are now trading was initially a grade three field with direct access to the public bridleway. This was a beneficial selling point for future development.

Planning consent was given for ten holiday lodges, and at a later date, a further ten lodges were granted permission - all surrounding a course fishing lake. The lake was dug before building commenced, clay-lined, and an artesian well was also installed for future protection. The lake has held water ever since and also supports an overflow 'mini river' system, meandering to our Still Rabbit lodges. Our water features are a wildlife haven and one of our most important features in promoting our short breaks and holidays.

Yellowtop Country Park specialises in providing family getaways and couples retreats alongside superb Carp fishing, which is included in your stay.

Still, Rabbit Lodges commenced fifteen years ago as an extension to Yellowtop Country Park. The concept was to provide the perfect getaway for couples - no children, no pets, a place to spend quality time together, creating memories that will last a lifetime.

A select development of seven bespoke lodges overlooking the meandering waterway feature.

The lodges were named after the rabbit breeds - Chinchilla, Havana, Beveren, Palomino, Bouscat, Argente and Britannia Petite. I thought this was slightly more sophisticated than Flopsy, Mopsy, Cottontail and Peter…

Yellowrush Lodge is the third aspect of our Park. This is our "Big House" on-site, its nickname during the building stage, but the name has stuck…This is our five-bedroomed family retreat for ten people—a special place to get together for that important special occasion.

Our three unique selling features:

Family getaways
Romantic breaks
Group retreats

The initial marketing of the park was via Hoseasons Holidays, but we soon developed our own marketing strategy, taking our own bookings via the Supercontrol booking system. Yellowtop was trading successfully.

Still Rabbit proved to be very popular. I designed each lodge around a particular romantic theme. This led to our returning guests 'trying out' each lodge to find their favourite.

The occupancy rate of the site is high, and we are open all year. We accommodate any length of stay, with any day arrival. This is something that our competitors do not always offer. We employ, on average, twelve people in the park. Our guests support the local businesses in the surrounding villages and the local tourist attractions.

In December 2019, I took over the park's running independently and became the sole owner.

At that moment, I realised that the park could now be everything I would wish it to be. It was one of the most important turning points in my life. Now was the time to take action.

I was fifty-five that December. I knew deep down that major changes needed to happen in my life. Important decisions had to be made. The business was going to be successful. After already achieving a significant mindset shift over the past five years, there now had to be another more significant shift to focus on in the long term. Looking at the bigger picture of running a business and understanding that today's decisions will impact the future. It was important and necessary to be open to change and to embrace new ideas and perspectives. Any change in life is the perfect opportunity to believe in yourself.

I was not the most self-confident person at this particular period of my life, but I knew that I had the determination and the stamina to keep going. One of the most exhilarating experiences is to get to the top of that hill or mountain, or to the top of the highest building in the vicinity, for that matter...the view from the top is worth the persistence!

The predominant factor in moving forward was knowing why I wanted to do what I was doing. I get huge satisfaction from reading the comment books in the lodges to find that our guests have had the most amazing time. I want to create places where people can escape everyday stresses and celebrate special occasions - where, even for one or two nights, you can leave with lasting memories. A place to 'get away from it all' focussed on going back to nature and the natural environment - all in the comfort of a luxury lodge.

I live 'on-site' now, and the family home was created at Yellowtop Country Park. I knew that I needed it and that it was a necessity in order to create my future, that I had to 'get away' from the site. I needed to escape from being confined to working and living my personal life in the same place.

In January 2020, I attended a one-day social media training day in Leeds, named 'Rockstar Social' organised by Big Business Events. Following this, I booked a three-day event in Birmingham on social media. I needed to put myself out of my comfort zone and also get my head around Facebook, Instagram and all things social media-related. I do remember putting myself to the front of the room, my heart pumping far too fast and telling everyone a little of my story. I also remember stating that along with the passion for the business, that life should be Fun! I joined up with my first business coach and mentor, Adam Stott, who founded Big Business Events. I became a member of Gold Circle, which is a part of Big Business Events.

To say that joining Gold Circle was a major milestone in my personal development is a complete understatement. My personal journey was about to begin. My travels down to Essex from Yorkshire would become a regular thing. Surrounding yourself with like-minded people is the best way to stay motivated and inspired. It is a supportive environment where you can share ideas and experiences. You are learning from people who have 'achieved' and who are working 'above you'.

To have a business coach where you 'deep dive' into all aspects of:

Sales,
Marketing,
Finances,
and everything in between is no easy task.

A coach is not there to 'do it for you'. You personally have to listen and take action on all the advice given.

I believe it is always essential to get your head around understanding the concepts of what you are learning before you outsource to another person or company.

Changes to the business were about to be instigated.

Sales is obviously an essential part of any business. Without sales, revenue cannot be generated, and the business will not sustain itself. Sales will provide feedback on the effectiveness of your marketing and product strategy. It will also provide insights into your customer preferences and needs, leading to all future product and marketing decisions.

With regard to the above - my journey began and is continuing…

The core product of Yellowtop Country Park and Still Rabbit Lodges is what sets us apart from other self-catering accommodations in the area.

The first and most important improvement I made to the site was to install WIFI throughout. This was a major decision that caused me a few sleepless nights! It was the first major financial decision that I needed to make to improve our guests' journey and future satisfaction. I sometimes felt like I was playing with Monopoly money! WIFI was essential to implement, and without it, the complaints from our guests would have increased. The cost implication completely freaked me out, but the recommendations and feedback we were getting left us with no choice. I chose the company to work with and made the decision to go ahead. Work commenced.

This was in March 2020. The whole of the road network between each lodge had to be dug up to install private WIFI on each property. Once work started, the realisation that the detrimental effect on our guests would be extreme also raised my cortisol levels!

But then, the lockdown arrived!

If there was ever a positive to happen out of COVID-19, this was the only positive for the business.

Subcontract work could carry on, and with no guests on-site, this major task was completed. This without doubt boosted our sales.

Being part of a coaching group paved the way to building some incredible relationships. My second major improvement was to update and reinvent our websites to increase sales. This was achieved by working with HC Media, as well as members of Gold Circle. The company now maintains our websites, works on our SEO, blogs, backlinks, and Google AdWords and has added us to Wikipedia. Being part of a coaching group opened the doors to having access to people you could work with and trust.

Branding was also something that I needed to reinvent. To have experts to show you the way was invaluable. We now feel that our branding promotes the elements of our business that are important to our future guests. These are our slogans for each aspect of our business…

Still Rabbit Lodges - 'Lose Yourself / Discover Yourself'
Yellowtop Country Park - 'Relax, after all, you deserve it'
Yellowrush Lodge - 'Creating memories together'

Social media is a massive part of the sales process. Our Facebook following was good, and I knew we already had our 'brand advocates'. We now needed to promote Instagram to obtain a new following to increase our sales. I outsourced this for a year to a digital marketer whom I also met via the coaching group.

We have now taken over our social media 'in-house', which has made everything so much more personal. Facebook and Instagram stories and posts are going out every day, and the communication with our guests has vastly improved. TikTok is now being promoted successfully, and at this moment in time, we are working on LinkedIn to aid our future sales development. Mailchimp promotes our seasonal special offers to entice our existing guests to return again and again.

By the way, I strongly believe that it is important to fully develop one aspect of social media before moving on to the next.

Sales, marketing and finance are such infinite subjects in any business. The learning will never come to an end. Picking up one golden nugget along the way from the coaches you are learning from can be one of the most transformational aspects of increasing sales in your business. It is in this atmosphere of learning that you can deeply connect with problems and challenges. The discipline of taking action is reinforced every day, week, and month; why wait when you can 'just do it'?

Do not be afraid to make mistakes and get things wrong. Life is a continuous learning curve, and we are expected to get things wrong repeatedly. Your coach is there to advise, but only one person can implement and take action to achieve your future goals. You cannot rely on anyone else to do it for you.

In the beginning, you can set small goals that are easily attainable. Goals can be set in the short term or the long term into the future. Set a large goal, and once committed in your mind, nothing will stop you from achieving it. The feeling of achieving your goal is amazing! You are worthy, and your destiny is in your hands…

One of the hardest achievements I have found to date is to create a team. You may have your goals, but to achieve them, it is important to have a team to help and support you along the way. The creation and development of Yellowtop Country Park and Still Rabbit Lodges would not be possible without our dedicated team over the years. Creating a team to work together and support each other has been no easy task and will continually require your time and support. I am under no illusion that there will be continuous ups and downs to the team's success 'vibes'. For whatever reason, life will dictate that the team will have to continually evolve with new people, personalities, and developments to work towards.

Communication is sooo important in all aspects of business. Without communication, there is little movement forward. Communication builds relationships...

Your network is your net worth.

So, so true.

Do not rely on one network. Branch out and find multiple network groups. Invest in your business outreach. Take as many opportunities that come your way as you can. Meeting new people, opening up new conversations and sharing problems will lead to positive moves forward. Continue to put yourself out of your comfort zone.

At this stage in my business development, Assets For Life has become a significant part of my network. Continuing my sales journey with Nick Staab has evolved due to the possibility of future business possibilities and decisions.

The realisation that sales are a never-ending challenge that will continue to be one of the most important skills to develop in all aspects of life and business is something that will always be at the forefront of all future goals.

The primary goal is to maintain the high standards we aim to achieve for our existing, future and repeat guests and brand advocates. Our business and our team are working together to serve our guests. Our guests' satisfaction dictates the future of the business. The aim for the future is to develop the park further. We are also in the midst of developing more partnerships with other businesses. We will be working alongside Martin House Hospice, as this is the charity I would most like to support, as children do not ask for or deserve what is happening to them. Our team will be involved in 'team challenges' to support our charity. As I have said previously, 'life should be fun', and the team will be present at the yearly 'charity ball' - this we can highly support by donating our romantic breaks at auction.

Yellowtop Country Park and Still Rabbit Lodges...

The ecology of our site in regards to nature and wildlife has matured to provide such a special place and biological environment for animals, birds, insects, plants and aquatic wildlife. Our runner ducks and duck families love to be fed from your decking. Roe deer now come and drink from the pond early in the morning, and bats and barn owls fly by at night. We have wild orchids growing in our hedgerows (shhh). From the grade three land that was on the ground in the beginning, the carbon imprint that we have established and the habitat that we have created is such a drastic change for the benefit of the ecology.

We have no light pollution in the middle of the Yorkshire countryside. You can sit back and look up at the stars. The environmental and ecological impact that we have had on the area is one of our top qualities, and we are very proud of it. It is a wildlife haven. From the twenty-seven-acre field twenty years ago, dreams are being fulfilled from all areas of the spectrum.

Sales, along with all other business strategies, will be the driving force to fulfil those future dreams...

DREAM BIG

P.S. I never dreamt that I would write a chapter in a book!
GOOD LUCK ON YOUR JOURNEY
HAVE FUN ALONG THE WAY
YOU DESERVE IT

My Top Tips:

Tip 1: Mindset and Positivity

Move yourself into a state of positivity. Focus on the present. Work on removing and evaluating past negatives in your life. Once you have a positive mindset, you can help others along life's journey. Focus on your mind, body and soul. Your story is created from now.

Tip 2: Network

Surround yourself and build relationships with people who have similar aspirations or have already attained their goals - to help and support you along the journey. Reach out and find multiple network groups. Invest in yourself and connect with motivated and energised people of the same mindset.

Tip 3: Goals

In the beginning, set small goals. Believe in yourself. Your continued mindset will ensure you attain your larger goals. Don't be afraid to get things wrong.

CHAPTER 16

Future in the Present

JOHN AYODELE

'The future you want is in your mindset and your routine.'

\- John Ayodele

In the summer of 2016, I had some friends over, and we had been going through a financial literacy workbook as we all wanted to be financially independent. As part of the exercise, we had to review our finances and cut where there was excess spending. For me, one of the areas I thought to cut spending was travelling.

We discussed this as a group, and I thought cycling to work would help by saving me over 50% - 70% of my transport spending, as well as helping to improve my health.

Guess what?

I don't even have a bicycle, I barely ride. To think of it, I learned to ride just before I turned 17. So, what am I supposed to do?

Anyway, we had an avid cyclist in the group who encouraged me, but I had some other folks who were concerned for me.

I decided to take a cycling road awareness course and got my bike and cycling gear. I remember clearly my first day cycling back from work, which was also the day I picked up my new bike. My instructor came along with me to pick it up and cycled with me to a location that I was comfortable with.

As my instructor left me to continue my journey, I hadn't gotten far at all before I had a minor incident whereby I learned how to do a front flip with my bike against my will.

Yes, you read that right. My bike and I flipped as I panicked due to a car coming behind me.

As soon as I landed on the floor, I picked myself up and went to a safe spot to dust myself off with what was left of my pride.

I had a choice to continue or just walk and push my bike along. Of course, I chose the former. Another decision had to be made when I got home.

Do I continue cycling to work, or do I stop and find other means to save money and stay healthy?

You can guess what happened.

Of course, I soldiered on with continuing cycling to work. I fell off my bike a number of times. I continued to show up on a daily basis by waking up at early hours to cycle into work.

And then there was the challenge of climbing the stairs.

I disliked doing this as it hurt loads, but I pressed on. With time, I got used to the pain of cycling and taking the stairs afterwards.

Over time, I also noticed I was able to have more money after bills were paid, which was the original plan!

There is nothing like meeting your goal after so much pain.

You may be wondering what this story has to do with the quote, '*The future you want is in your mindset and your routine.*'

It has everything to do with it because everything we need or want starts in our mind, and then the actions which are our routine will determine if we achieve it or not.

I had to start with my 'Why' in my mind and then decide what actions needed to be taken. I then broke this down on a daily basis, which made up my routine, and eventually, I achieved my desired future.

In my opinion, every time we are faced with a setback in life, we have a major decision to make that relates to either continuing or stopping.

My Mindset and My Why

Knowing your *why*? It would help you in overcoming the challenges to both current and future. It also helps you to make decisions that add to your cause.

When you set out to do anything in life, you spend time pondering on it. In the process of pondering on it, you identify the core of what you want to do.

The core is your 'Why?' It forms the foundation which your mindset about what you want to do is built upon.

It's like building a house. The type of house you want to build will determine the foundation you lay for it. In other words, your 'Why' will determine what you do and how you do it. It is the part you keep referring back to while you're on your journey to achieve what you set out to do.

It also determines your mindset to achieve your goals. Before your goal becomes a reality, you first have to conceive and achieve it in your mind. Your mind arrives at the future before your body. Where your mind goes, your body eventually follows. It is crucial to focus on your mind as it's where life is determined.

It is where you decide if you can or can't, just as Henry Ford said,

"Whether you think you can or you think you can't, you're right."

Before I started cycling, I had to see myself riding to work, saving money and being healthier. That was the first thing I had in my mind. My mind was already at the end of the journey before I began to see the manifestation in my body and, of course, my account.

Imagine if I had not made up my mind before I started cycling to work that I wasn't going to quit no matter what and also constantly remind myself, 'Why?' I was doing this. If I hadn't done this, I would've easily quit, considering the challenges I faced.

Always take time to know your mind about whatever you want to do. Once this is sorted out, it's easier to proceed.

Baby Steps and Routine

Once you decide what it is you want to do, then you make up a plan to achieve it and break it down into what I call baby steps. These Baby Steps make up your routine, which leads to the future you want.

If you really want to sustain and make a long-term difference in life, you have to start with baby steps. Baby steps on a daily basis, make bigger steps that form your routines. I believe this is the difference between ordinary and extraordinary people.

Imagine every day I wake up to jog on the spot for 5 minutes, and I do this for 30 days in a month. Five multiplied by 30 days equals 150 minutes per month.

It may not seem like much, but by doing this time and time again over a year, that's 1800 minutes. That's definitely not small, right? Just as the quote below.

'Little drops of water, little grains of sand make the mighty ocean and the beauteous land.' – Julia A. Carney.

For me, I decided I would like to cycle into work three to five days a week. I broke it down for a number of days. Then, I started off with two to three days (remember, baby steps).

Once my body was used to it, I increased it gradually until I reached five days a week. It was easier for me to sustain this over a long time as the baby steps I took made up my routine. I wasn't trying out a totally new routine. Instead, I replaced taking the train or the bus with cycling. Therefore, I didn't have to have this entirely new routine.

I have always been someone who gradually eases back into any form of routine even though I can do more. My aim is always to sustain whatever I'm doing for a long period of time. This has worked for me over the years and still does. Can you imagine someone who had a cycling accident and was hospitalised for a number of days to weeks? Would you advise that individual to go back to cycling as soon as they are discharged from the hospital? Of course not, as they'll need to gradually build their strength back before being able to cycle like they used to. If they try to do more sooner than they should, they risk hurting themselves more than their initial injury. So why then do we rush to get back into things when we fall off our chosen path? Our routines are similar to this scenario, and if you take baby steps to get back into it, you have more chances to sustain and improve it.

The Future / Goal Accomplished

By now, you're wondering what happens after you become clear about your 'Why?', your mindset, and baby steps. Well, you arrive at the future you want.

It doesn't happen overnight. Just like Dr Phil McGraw said, 'Life's a marathon, not a sprint.'

It takes discipline and commitment to arrive here and more discipline to stay here or go beyond.

I remember when I realised I'd accomplished my goal of being healthy and saving money. I was over the moon about it. I even wrote a post about it and had some comments from others who said I inspired them to do the same. Can you imagine how this made me feel? I was inspired to do and be more. Inspiring others to action brings some form of fulfilment like no other.

Imagine if I hadn't taken the steps I took. The future I wanted would just be a wish. There are people in my circle of influence who would not accomplish what they should sooner because I haven't taken the necessary steps. just like Sam Adeyemi said, 'I have discovered that when you work on an idea, it produces other ideas.'

Think of your future as an idea that gives birth to other ideas when implemented. By implementing it, others get creative and bring their own ideas to fruition.

Imagine a music band which has a drummer, guitarist, bassist and pianist. The Pianist plays some chord progression, and the other band members get ideas and begin creating parts that suit the progression. If the pianist hadn't played the chord progression, the others wouldn't get such ideas.

This is similar to an individual taking action towards their future through their daily routine. By doing so, they inspire others to get creative.

Wanting a better future for yourself and working on it helps others have a reference point. In our mission to be better ourselves, we help others to be better. Don't wait until you're excellent. Instead, start with baby steps today, and your tomorrow will thank you for it.

Always remember that your future is in your today!

My Top Tips:

Tip 1: Never start something without knowing your 'Why' and having a crystal-clear mind about it.

Tip 2: In anything you do, start with baby steps so you sustain it.

Tip 3: Remember to help others along the way, as well as after you have arrived at your desired future.

CHAPTER 17

The Revelation of Sales: A Path to Financial Security and Empowering Others

KEIRON NGUYEN

'To get something you never had, you have to do something you've never done.'

- Unknown

Motivated by a fervent desire to carve out a prosperous future for my children, I ventured into the captivating realm of property investment.

The allure of securing a passive income stream and gaining increased time freedom beckoned irresistibly.

Yet, in this odyssey, an unexpected revelation surfaced—the indispensable role of sales in any business endeavour. Initially rooted in the pursuit of financial security, the appeal of property investment expanded to embrace the intricate dance of salesmanship.

Navigating the complex landscape of real estate, I discerned that effective sales strategies were not merely advantageous but fundamentally crucial for success.

This newfound awareness reshaped my perspective, illuminating the symbiotic relationship between property ventures and the artistry of sales.

As I aspired to fortify the foundations for a secure future, it became evident that mastering the nuances of salesmanship constituted an integral part of the journey toward prosperity in the dynamic world of property investment. This realisation planted the seed of ambition, propelling me further into the synergistic intersection of real estate and the artful science of sales.

In the course of my pursuit of property opportunities, serendipity led me to a transformative moment—the "Assets for Life" webinar hosted by Nick Staab. Initially drawn to the event for its two property-related bootcamps, it was the unexpected revelation of the third bootcamp, titled 'Elite Sales Specialist' and personally conducted by Nick Staab, that seized my focus.

This webinar became a pivotal juncture in my journey. Nick Staab's expertise in property investment was evident, but it was his emphasis on the art and science of sales in the 'Elite Sales Specialist' bootcamp that proved to be a game-changer. The webinar provided insights into the nuanced world of salesmanship within the context of property ventures, unveiling strategies that went beyond the conventional approaches.

This unexpected twist expanded my horizons, revealing the interconnectedness of effective sales techniques with the success of property endeavours. Nick Staab's guidance became a beacon, illuminating the path towards not just property prosperity but a holistic mastery that integrated sales acumen into the very fabric of my approach. The "Assets for Life" webinar, and particularly the "Elite Sales Specialist"bootcamp, became the catalyst that reshaped my understanding, setting the stage for a more comprehensive and impactful journey into the realm of property investment.

Prior to encountering the 'Elite Sales Specialist' concept, I, like many, harboured a stereotypical view of salespeople as somewhat dubious characters solely fixated on extracting money. This preconceived notion painted them as individuals employing slick tactics to close deals, leaving customers feeling manipulated. However, the revelation of the 'Elite Sales Specialist' shattered these stereotypes and ushered in a paradigm shift.

The concept unveiled a profound and transformative perspective on the role and purpose of a salesperson. Far from the negative stereotypes, it portrayed sales as an art form, emphasising genuine connection, understanding, and value creation. The 'Elite Sales Specialist' concept challenged the notion that salesmanship is merely transactional; instead, it showcased it as a holistic and collaborative process. It emphasised the importance of fostering relationships, addressing needs, and providing authentic solutions.

This newfound understanding not only debunked the misconceptions surrounding salespeople but also elevated the profession to a level of respectability. The 'Elite Sales Specialist' concept redefined the true essence of a salesperson, portraying them as trusted advisors, problem solvers, and partners in a mutually beneficial journey. This revelation not only reshaped my perception but also underscored the profound impact a skilled and ethical salesperson can have in creating value and building lasting relationships.

Transforming into an 'Elite Sales Specialist' marked a shift in my approach, placing a premium on the art of problem-solving. Immersed in the dynamic realm of property management, particularly within the domain of serviced accommodations, my primary focus became addressing the multifaceted challenges confronted by landlords. Instead of merely pushing products or services, my role evolved into a strategic partnership centred on resolving the real-world issues they grappled with.

In navigating the intricate landscape of property investment, I became adept at identifying pain points and tailoring solutions. The economic climate posed unique challenges, and my mission was clear: empower landlords to overcome these obstacles. My expertise is aimed at not just increasing their income but also orchestrating strategies to attract professional tenants. By doing so, I offered a comprehensive remedy to the struggles landlords faced, transcending the traditional sales narrative.

This problem-solving orientation not only distinguished me as an 'Elite Sales Specialist' but also solidified the value proposition of my services. The art of addressing and resolving the genuine concerns of prospects became the cornerstone of my approach, fostering trust and long-term partnerships. As I adeptly navigated the complexities of property management, the role transcended conventional sales; it became a purposeful endeavour, where success wasn't merely measured in transactions but in the tangible, positive impact on the lives and businesses of those I served.

In the realm of the "Elite Sales Specialist," the allure lies in the creation of a genuine win-win scenario. As I embarked on this journey, the beauty unfolded in the mutually beneficial nature of the interactions. Acting as a conduit for landlords to maximise their property's income potential became a cornerstone, not just for the growth of my own business but also for the empowerment of landlords in expanding their enterprises.

The essence of this symbiotic relationship extended beyond conventional sales dynamics. It wasn't merely about closing deals but creating value on both ends. By meticulously understanding the unique needs and goals of landlords, I could tailor solutions that not only optimised their property investments but also propelled their financial success. This approach, rooted in collaboration rather than coercion, defined the true spirit of being an 'Elite Sales Specialist'.

The positive impact reverberated, illustrating the transformative power of ethical and strategic salesmanship. This approach not only elevated my standing in the industry but also forged lasting partnerships based on trust and mutual benefit. The

'Elite Sales Specialist' role, far from a traditional sales archetype, became a testament to the potential for sales to be a force for positive change, showcasing that when done with integrity and foresight, sales can genuinely be a win-win scenario for all parties involved.

In February, my enthusiasm peaked as I eagerly immersed myself in a transformative three-day bootcamp in Essex. The intensity of those days paled in comparison to the extraordinary content presented, reshaping my perception of sales, and crystallising the essence of becoming an 'Elite Sales Specialist'.

This experience was a profound journey into the heart of effective salesmanship. It opened my eyes to a new understanding of the role—a dynamic blend of serving people with genuine needs and ensuring a harmonious fit for collaboration. The curriculum extended beyond conventional sales tactics, introducing a meticulous 7-step serving system that became the backbone of my approach.

The bootcamp emphasised the significance of aligning offerings with genuine client needs. It wasn't merely about selling but about serving—providing solutions that genuinely addressed the challenges and desires of potential clients. The qualification process became a crucial filter, ensuring a mutual fit that would foster meaningful and successful collaborations.

This newfound understanding transcended the stereotypical image of sales, revealing it as a purposeful endeavour centred on service and value creation. The bootcamp not only equipped me with practical strategies but instilled a deeper philosophy, transforming the very core of my approach as I embraced the role of an 'Elite Sales Specialist'.

Empowered by the profound insights gleaned from the transformative bootcamp experience, I wholeheartedly embraced the mantle of an 'Elite Sales Specialist' within my property management ventures. Armed with a fresh perspective, I embarked on each prospect interaction with an authentic eagerness to comprehend their unique pain points.

My approach became a purposeful journey of understanding, transcending the transactional aspects of sales to delve into the intricate nuances of clients' needs. Armed with the belief that success is a shared venture, I sought not only to address concerns but to craft bespoke solutions that would yield mutual benefits. The 7-step serving system learned during the bootcamp became my guiding framework, ensuring a methodical and empathetic approach to every interaction.

This approach wasn't just about securing deals; it was about fostering meaningful partnerships. I became attuned to the rhythm of collaboration, aligning my offerings with the genuine needs of each prospect. The role of an 'Elite Sales Specialist' became a dynamic synergy of service and strategy, where success was measured not just in transactions but in the tangible positive impact on both their business and mine. As I applied these lessons, the art of salesmanship transformed into a purposeful and mutually enriching endeavour within the realm of property management.

In the face of soaring living costs and escalating rates, the conventional buy-to-let model for landlords found itself rendered less profitable. Recognising the shifting landscape, I sought to unleash untapped potential by pivoting towards the serviced accommodations property management model. This strategic move wasn't just a response to industry changes but a proactive means of providing landlords with a pathway to thrive amidst challenges.

The serviced accommodations approach became a beacon of adaptability in the current economic climate. It wasn't merely about finding alternatives; it was about maximising the income potential of properties while addressing the evolving needs of the market. By navigating landlords through this transformative shift, I offered more than a service – it was a solution tailored to the times.

In embracing the serviced accommodations model, landlords could unlock a realm of possibilities, optimising their investments for heightened profitability. This shift wasn't just a transactional adjustment; it represented a strategic response to the changing landscape, empowering landlords to not only weather challenges but to thrive in an environment of constant flux. In unleashing the potential within this evolving property management paradigm, I facilitated a transition that not only addressed immediate concerns but positioned landlords for sustained success in a dynamic and unpredictable real estate landscape.

Embarking on my path as an 'Elite Sales Specialist', my commitment to fostering prosperity persists. In the realm of property management, I dedicate myself to serving landlords with innovative solutions that transcend conventional boundaries. My focus extends beyond mere transactions; it is a concerted effort to nurture sustained growth and provide a foundation for financial security.

As I navigate this journey, the objective is clear: to contribute to a brighter future for both myself and the landlords under my care. This involves not only adapting to the evolving landscape but proactively shaping it through strategic and empathetic salesmanship. By empowering landlords with the tools to thrive in dynamic markets, I aspire to create a future defined by mutual growth and success—a testament to the transformative power of an 'Elite Sales Specialist' in the realm of property management.

In culmination, my venture into property sales has been nothing short of a transformative odyssey, reshaping my perceptions of the profession. Embracing the role of an 'Elite Sales Specialist' has illuminated the profound influence that strategic and ethical salesmanship can wield, not just in fostering my business growth but in cultivating the prosperity of the clients I am privileged to serve.

This chapter in my life represents more than a career shift; it's a trajectory towards financial security, time freedom, and the empowering of others within the dynamic landscape of property investment. The lessons learned, particularly during the intensive bootcamp experience, have become the guiding principles shaping my approach—centred on a 7-step serving system and the art of problem-solving.

As I stand at the threshold of this journey, the excitement of the unknown beckons. The prospect of navigating the complexities of property sales with the mindset of an 'Elite Sales Specialist' fuels my enthusiasm for the road ahead. This is not just a professional pursuit; it's a commitment to a future defined by growth, empowerment, and the continual evolution of my understanding of the profound impact sales can have in shaping a prosperous and fulfilling life.

My Top Tips:

Tip 1: Surround yourself with the right people.

Tip 2: If in a room, I want to be the dumbest person in there so I can learn from the smartest people.

Tip 3: Find a mentor to help guide you and also someone to hold you accountable.

CHAPTER 18

Life Is All About the Choices We Make

MARK TIPPER

'Success is not final; failure is not fatal: it is the courage to continue that counts.'

- Winston Churchill

I AM CONSTANTLY TRYING to better myself for my family's future so I can provide for them and for my future grandchildren and create intergenerational wealth. My aim in life is to have multiple streams of income with a combination of businesses and properties that give both quality and value for money to customers, tenants, and guests alike.

I have never been in a position where money is no object and have constantly worried about having 'too much month left at the end of the money'! My dream is to be able to walk into practically any shop and not have to worry about the cost or whether I can afford an item or not. Isn't this everyone's dream?

My first sales experience was when I was 15 and still at school. I managed to secure myself a Saturday job at McDonald's, working on the tills at a local McDonald's down Southend seafront. The job involved taking orders, dealing with money (I laugh as I recall that as I do not remember people using credit/debit cards back in 1999), gathering customers' food orders and presenting them with a smile, hoping they would be happy. The majority were okay, but you got the odd one or two that would kick off about something. If this is what selling is (dealing with the public), then I would not choose it as a career path, I thought.

When I was at school, I never knew what I wanted to do after finishing my exams. Instead of work experience, we had a mock interview day. We had to put down two types of jobs that we were interested in. I put down engineering as someone once said that if you like making stuff with your hands, then engineering is a good thing to do. I also enjoyed art, so I thought I could be a graphic designer. Anyway, the interview the school managed to get me was at a local engineering firm that made crew seats and other aerospace components, mainly for Boeing, Cessna, and Embraer aircraft. It was explained how I could perform better to improve my chances of securing a job, and I was also informed that there was an opening for apprenticeship places due to start in September after the summer holidays. Needless to say, I knew what I needed to do and how to do it. I went for the interview and got one of the three places available. I could earn money while going to college five days a week. I would get £113 a week and the weekends to myself, whilst all my other friends went on to college and then had to get weekend jobs to earn a little bit of money.

I generally enjoyed my job and had a fantastic opportunity of being chosen to set up a £250,000 all-singing, all-dancing 9-Axis machine, which involved a programming course in Worcester with a fellow employee. We had to program everything from scratch and get parts off quicker and off the machine complete, whereas before, they went on between two to nine different machines to complete the same job. It was very successful and an outstanding achievement. Once this project was completed, the same jobs kept running on it with no more room for any new work, so things became a bit like Groundhog Day again. I was constantly thinking there must be more to life than this, and I was fed up with being stuck within the same four walls in an engineering factory that was sweltering in summer and blistering cold in winter. I worked near a roller shutter door by the stores for just shy of 17 years. The guys on the shop floor were some of the greatest people you could ever wish to meet, although the management was somewhat questionable. I was comfortable, but I wanted something more. As the saying goes,

> *'A comfort zone is a beautiful place – but nothing ever grows there.'*
>
> - Anonymous.

Trying to get out of engineering was challenging at the time. I could have got a job in a neighbouring town doing the same thing for more money, but after taking into account the travelling time, petrol money and wear and tear on the car, I wasn't going to be much better off, plus I wanted something more, something different. I wanted to be able to use my engineering qualifications and skills to do something different rather than starting over in a completely different field, as by this time, I had a mortgage to pay. I couldn't afford to take any drop in pay as my girlfriend at the time was training to be a solicitor. I tried on several occasions to get out and into something different. Still, nothing seemed to be worth leaving for with the amount of pay or opportunity to progress, or I would receive the 'Dear Mark' letters telling me that I was unsuccessful, we'll keep your details in case other opportunities arise, thanks for trying.

My last year at the engineering company at the age of 32, resulted in me getting a promotion to become a programmer, programming CNC machines on computer software rather than on the machines on the shop floor, which involved dressing smarter and sitting in an office on a computer for the majority of the time, with a bit of proving out programmes on the shop floor to make sure the machines did what they were supposed to do by producing the part correctly and not smashing anything up!

So you can get an idea, just picture my boss who wore his shirt rarely tucked in around his waist and trousers; he looked like the scruffiest person in the company, had a shiny bald head with wisps of hair around the side and glasses that had been repaired with tape. One day, he called my team leader and me into his office and shut the door. "What's going on here?" I said. It turned out to be a meeting to discuss my performance and how I wasn't meeting their expectations. My boss told me I wasn't programming jobs quickly enough, and my team leader, who I thought had my back as we were pretty friendly, threw me under the bus and agreed with everything my boss said. I explained that the software was constantly crashing, causing any unsaved work to be lost, and they knew this but didn't want to take action. It didn't sway them. Being a conscientious worker, this actually took the wind out of my sails. I was distraught by the news that I was not performing and had taken longer than I should have on some complex parts. I took some time off work following this and was signed off with what is called 'low mood', but it felt like depression. This really didn't suit me. Something had to change.

At the age of 33, I found two highly regarded tooling companies that were looking for an Area Sales Manager, and these were the most exciting opportunities that I had come across with excellent basic pay and the opportunity to earn something called commission. My girlfriend helped with mock interview questions and even travelled to Birmingham with me for moral support in an old, most basic bright blue one-litre Vauxhall Corsa with wind-down handle windows, crappy wheel trims, and an awful interior. It shook as soon as it went over 50 mph. It was as if it came from the Inbetweeners if you've ever seen it.

I even went to visit my grandad in Surrey to work on and practise my presentation that I had prepared on DJ-ing, which is my greatest passion, as the companies required a presentation on something completely non-work related. My grandad had built and sold a profitable business before he retired and wanted to help, which I gratefully obliged.

I had interviews arranged for both of them but took the first one after being offered the job at the end of the second interview without even visiting the other company and couldn't wait to get started.

I remember the first day, which was so exciting for me. My new boss picked me up from my home in Southend-on-Sea and drove to Birmingham to collect my first company car, which I inherited from the last Area Sales Manager. It was a black Mazda with very few miles on the clock and had just been fully valeted. I remember feeling on top of the world as it felt like I was picking up a brand-new car as it was the newest car I had ever had the pleasure of driving, a massive upgrade to the old Vauxhall Corsa!

I really enjoyed my second sales role; it put me right out of my comfort zone, but this was how I learned so much. It was a combination of managing existing accounts and cold calling to receive more accounts to manage in the future. I actually enjoyed cold calling and the thrill of potentially closing brand-new work.

This taught me far more than just the product and how to apply it; this role taught me how to deal with customers, from people on the shop floor in a factory, right the way up to senior management and business owners, how to present solutions using presentations on PowerPoint and how to listen to people and read between the lines. All this had what I wanted to do and feel like I was born to do, and that was to help people, whether that was saving two of the most important things in any business, in my opinion, and that is time and money at the same time helping my employer and myself to commission. The commission was a monthly bonus of up to £500 if you were hitting the same figures as the previous year, and if you managed to grow on the previous year, then you would receive 9% on the growth at the end of the year, this was your January bonus incentive which was great as I was generally most skint after Christmas. Even when times were hard, and I knew I wasn't growing the business due to factors outside of my control, such as my largest customer going into administration, I couldn't help but do my best. Giving up wasn't an option for me. It just meant I needed to try harder to potentially set myself up for the next year and grow, helping both customers and the business. After all, that was what I was being paid for.

When the big 'C' virus came in 2020, the company lost millions in profits as everyone was told to stay at home and work from home if possible. In our industry, people would not be taking machines home like they did their computers. They needed to be on-site, so very little tooling was being purchased apart from the customers who were staying open to make parts for ventilators. As lockdowns started to ease off, the company advised that they would be altering the bonus structure so that you were not being judged on your previous year when Covid was about but the year before. This made it practically impossible to earn any bonus, so I knew what I had to do: move on somewhere else.

I briefly moved to another tooling company as a Technical Sales Manager that specialised in cutting composites and carbon fibre with tooling made at their factory in Coventry for just two months. I would have stayed but was approached by my old team leader from when I was on the shop floor, who was now the sales director at a machine tool company that was an agent for several different machine brands. 'This is it', I thought, I had followed the natural progression from the shop floor, programming, tool sales and now machine sales! Machine sales came with the same basic salary but with much larger commissions: capital expenditure and commission on everything sold in your area.

It was a great start, staying away whilst training with the new boss for the first four days and going out for dinner every night. The owner of the company and his wife even came out with us one evening, which was a nice touch. When machines were being sold, everything was great, but when they weren't, the boss would start interrogating me, calling me up and asking where my next machine sale was coming from, and for some reason, when he used to ask me, I would panic, and then my mind would go totally blank! Thirteen machines sold in the space of twelve months, which was pretty good going, but the sales weren't consistent enough for the boss, and he had sold two of them because the customer went straight to him as they had a relationship. Another four machines were a tip-off from our finance broker, and even though I visited them at the right time and worked to get them over the line, he still didn't see the value in my efforts. The pressure was intense, which was okay, but he would start shouting down the phone if we lost an order to a competitor. He thought he was one of the best salesmen in his field, but he never used to be able to give me the necessary help and guidance when things were a little slow. He just looked at customer visits on our CRM and said it was good. I was visiting all these customers but couldn't understand why I wasn't selling more. It didn't make sense to him.

The day then came when the straw that broke the camel's back came. We had a customer coming to visit our showroom for the second time. The first time he visited he didn't commit. My boss still didn't believe the customer was going to order this time around either. He did though, and he was happy until the customer left. Then he pulled me into the meeting room for a dressing down. Another customer had apparently just ordered a machine with someone else because I advised that our delivery time was too long for the customer to wait, and he needed a machine in a matter of weeks and not months. I explained that we had not even discussed delivery, but it was as if he didn't believe me. So what should have been a good day ended up with me driving home very angry. I called the customer the next day to see what was going on, and they hadn't even placed an order, so my boss's information was incorrect. Not even a sorry!

I spoke with my father on the way home, and he explained that as he turned 67 years old the following year, he would either try to sell the Estuary Fire Protection business or allow me to work for him and take it over when the time suited. Only then could I see a new pathway away from engineering altogether and finally own and scale my own business, become my own boss, and have total control of my destiny.

Since joining in 2022, I have taken the work ethic, learnt skills & passion into growing a business and rarely look back. I had been putting off the Elite Sales Bootcamp as I booked it whilst working for my last boss. He wouldn't let me take it as paid as he didn't deem it necessary and would teach me how he became successful, but we know how that turned out. I had a minimal holiday (the most limited ever) so I was unable to attend, and taking several sick days to complete the course did not sit right with me, so I had to book it off with my father. He is very old school and told me that he had done a day of sales training before, and they told him to get friendly with the lady in reception and send emails. It is such an out-of-date approach I almost can't believe that there was ever a course on this. It was probably called the Sleazy Sales Course or words to that effect.

Since completing the boot camp and joining the Elite Sales Academy, I have further progressed my skills. It has also given me great ideas that are needed to help bring a company into the 21st Century and put the systems in place ready to scale the business. I even have a cold calling script now where I only ever had an opening of a script in the past for other job roles. This is helping me get further into conversations and uncover more information than just winging it like I had been for the past seven years!

At present, for my day-to-day work, I am a director for the family fire protection company that covers mainly Essex, Kent, Hertfordshire, and London. I provide refill and service extinguishers, test fire alarms, supply signage, survey premises and arrange fire risk assessments. Although fire protection and extinguishers aren't the most exciting products to many, the taking over of a business, growing and scaling appeals massively to me, as it should do to any aspiring entrepreneur. When I first started, I could almost instantly see where I could add value to the business, and my door-to-door knocking experience came in very handy indeed. This was different in the sense that every commercial premise is now an opportunity, whereas I used only to visit engineering factories, but this is no longer the case. It has stood me in good stead, and now we are at a point where my father only works when absolutely necessary, and I am so busy that I no longer have the time to cold call. We are at the point where we need to expand, so watch this space!

My Top Tips:

Tip 1: Never give up; we only fail when we quit, and failures are learning as long as we learn from them. Look towards others who are a little further down the road than yourself and, even better, learn from their mistakes.

Tip 2: Keep an open mind and keep learning in life, 'When you're green, you're growing; when you're ripe, you rot.' - Ray Kroc. I initially thought that I would finish learning subjects once I finished college. How wrong was I? I actually enjoy learning by attending courses, seminars and networking events more than whatever I did in school and college.

Tip 3: Don't let people tell you can't, even if they're only trying to protect you. I've had this from some of my nearest and dearest. It's your life, and you only get one crack at it, so live it!

CHAPTER 19

Selling Is Loving

SANDRA WOOLVEN

'Selling is listening, loving and living limitlessly.

We sell all day long to those around us and, most importantly, to ourselves.

Every conversation is a sales pitch.

Conscious, empathetic & effortless selling opens the door to freedom.'

- Sandra Woolven

'You could go into sales.'

My mother's matter-of-fact words as I was contemplating my career options at 17; she might as well have dropped a bombshell in front of me. I looked at her with all the contempt and disgust that a 17-year-old can direct towards their parents. Was she out of her mind? All I could think of was those door-to-door sales reps who rarely failed to convince my parents to buy all manner of things that they did not necessarily need.

In all honesty, she attempted to point out that sales in businesses was completely different to what I thought of as sales, but her words fell on deaf ears. That steel door was firmly shut, tightly locked, with the key nowhere to be seen.

However, have you ever noticed how life has a way of bringing you full circle, back to that thing you swore you would never do? Well, it certainly came back at me. It turns out that the door was not as impenetrable as I had thought.

Trilingual sales administrator – that was my first actual job after finishing a degree in languages and post-graduate in education. It was followed by UK sales administrator, export sales administrator and export sales account manager.

I hear you… Irony… In my defence, I will say that none of these jobs was actually what I would, at the time, have defined as selling – no pushy sales pitch, no trying to convince someone to buy something they did not need, no lengthy negotiations. I was mostly looking after existing customers and handling their orders.

Fast-forward another decade, spent in the trenches of British schools, and the time had come for the mid-life career change – not a crisis, but a heart-led desire to make a difference in another way, brought on by an event which had affected my family. Passionately and enthusiastically, I trained as a Rapid Transformational Therapist. My only focus: becoming a phenomenal therapist, one who could help clients overcome long-standing, limiting issues quickly.

Little did I know that this part was the fun and easy part, little did I realise what was looming ahead, and little did I appreciate the struggle that would come next. Holding my shiny new certificate, I hit the proverbial wall – I now had to sell my services. This time, we were talking about 'real, actual' selling!!! In order to be able to help people using my expertise, I had to first find and convince said people to buy what I offered.

The ink had not quite finished drying on my therapist certificate when the gloomy reality dawned on me, weighing heavily – I was going to have to step into the uncomfortable and distinctly icky world of sales.

Since the universe does not just have a way to land on you the very thing you swore you would never do but also a way to handle it, a small glimmer of hope shone in a suddenly very dark world. A couple of months previously, whilst starting my serviced accommodation business, fate had put on my path Nick Staab, an expert in heart-led selling.

In getting to know him, I had come to realise that sales was not exactly the way I had always pictured it. I had also observed first-hand that his amazing skills in the art of selling products and services were transferrable to different aspects of his life, both personal and professional, and undoubtedly accounted for a large part of his overall success.

Nick became my guide as I reluctantly dipped my toes into these uncharted, turbulent waters while doing my best to put aside my old negative feelings about selling. He kindly invited me to join one of his bootcamps, and after a few months of further struggling, I decided the time had come to seize the bull by the horn and see what the hype around selling was all about.

What followed was a life-transforming event, where I not only met a heart-led family of entrepreneurs, all eager to use their life experiences to help others, but also finally understood the psychology behind empathetic selling. As a therapist, coach and special needs teacher who had spent many years 'selling' mathematics and other subjects to struggling children, I could see that his approach made complete sense. I also instinctively felt the potential power of the application of these principles to other areas of life like school, family, relationships, work, etc. What Nick was selling was, in my view, a communication course in empathetic listening and loving, in brief, the secret to happy, connected, successful living.

I could already imagine the impact of mastering the skills on his level in such a way that it became a genuine, automatic and natural way of approaching and communicating with everyone in my life.

We sell our ideas, our opinions, our thoughts, our observations, our wishes, our requests, our desires, our dreams to our family members, to our friends, to our colleagues and, often unconsciously, to ourselves. Selling is just effective communication and negotiation.

My son dryly dubbed it 'the art of manipulation' - I laughingly conceded, provided that we both agreed that 'manipulation', in its purest sense, simply denotes skilful handling without any inherent negativity. After all, encouraging your children to establish healthy bedtime routines and eat nutritiously, motivating students to embrace learning, inspiring partners to display greater affection and care, encouraging managers to adopt innovative ideas, persuading employers to recognise your suitability for a role, or fostering kinder interactions among people hardly appears as a grave ethical dilemma. It's essentially the art of persuasion.

And, for the big one, how about being such a natural at selling that you can convince yourself to do those things you have been postponing for a lifetime? How about the ability to spot and reroute negative self-talk thanks to your selling skills? As far as I see it, mastering the art of selling is mastering the art of truly living.

In the world of personal development, 'knowing your why' is a recurrent theme and is usually considered the starting point and the most important part of any action you undertake. Without why, there is no what, who, where, when or how. If you are just doing something because someone told you to do so without truly understanding why you are doing it, you will most likely experience resistance, struggle or even failure, so I felt it was essential to begin my story with what I view as the 'why' behind learning to sell.

The other reason is that buying is emotional, and emotion always wins over logic. We like to think of ourselves as reasonable, sensible, logical beings, but neuroscience points to the contrary.

Our choices and decisions are primarily motivated by how we feel. As such, connecting emotionally with our potential buyers, relating to them, helping them to imagine how the end result will feel, whether we are trying to convince a child to eat carrots or someone to buy a service, this stirring of positive, desired feelings will have an undeniably considerable impact on the outcome, both qualitatively and quantitatively.

Telling your six-year-old that eating their carrots is healthy is unlikely to yield the desired result, but making a game of it or telling them it will give them a superpower will create positive emotions, which will significantly increase the chances of them eating said carrots.

Similarly, selling your coaching by telling a client that you are a fantastic coach, that you definitely can help them overcome their struggle or that you use cutting-edge techniques will not have the same impact as making the potential client feel heard or as helping them identify why they want this and how they will feel when they have it.

This leads us neatly to the importance of empathy. No matter who you are selling to, be it your partner, your boss or a major client, they will only be truly open to considering what you are selling if they feel that you have taken the time to understand their personal standpoint, the uniqueness of their situation, the particularity of their struggle. They need to feel important, to know that their feelings matter and to feel like you genuinely care about them.

The most likely obstacle to this will be a pressing desire to close the deal, to make the sale, to win. When the other party senses that you are pushing your own agenda hard, they are no longer sure that you truly have their best interests at heart but think that it is all about you and about what you want. Once the dominant feeling is one of upmanship, you are more likely to lose them than win them over.

Honest interest is essential because most people naturally feel disingenuity and will automatically erect an invisible barrier. With this in mind, how can you create empathy and connection?

This is where selling becomes about loving. You will be glad to know that I am not suggesting that you should demonstrate deep, abiding love for each potential client. However, showing genuine interest in them out of heart-felt kindness will make all the difference. Engage your curious, childlike mind. Look for something that matters to the other person, and if you happen to hit on something that you can relate to easily, even better. Alternatively, it might be that you can relate their struggle or dream to someone else you have served or helped. Show that you care, that you want to help and that you are serving with true kindness.

It might help to remember that in doing this, you are also acting out of love for yourself. In showing true consideration for what matters to them, the law of reciprocity will automatically open them up to being willing to consider your point, your idea, and your needs. This will, therefore, increase your chances of getting you that sale that you wanted, the holiday with your partner, a well-deserved promotion or simply a bit of peace and quiet at home. So, in demonstrating concern for the other party's feelings and needs, you are really serving and loving yourself.

Ethical, successful selling is a gift that keeps on giving – you are not just caring about the client or yourself, you are also spreading the love. That sale, holiday, promotion, peace and quiet – who do they also benefit? All those you love. Maybe you are earning more money, meaning a bigger house, a luxury car, a brand-new wardrobe or a holiday around the world, or maybe the atmosphere at home is so much more harmonious and loving that everyone starts to feel happier and act kinder towards one another. Selling is loving and quality living.

One caveat – make sure that you are passionate about whatever you are selling, be it an idea, a product or a service. Loving is also important in that regard. To authentically sell something based on the premise that it will serve the receiver, you must believe 100% in the quality of what you sell, in its value and potential as a true act of kindness. If your heart is not in what you are selling, you will considerably decrease your chances of closing the deal; you will lose credibility and also risk your own well-being by repeatedly going against what feels right for you.

Selling is listening, listening to your inner voice, to your gut instinct about what you sell and, most importantly, listening to the other person. Nick Staab recommends a ratio of 80% listening to 20% talking. As a talker myself, this creates an interesting challenge. However, I have found that what matters is the quality of your listening, a vastly underrated and underdeveloped skill.

Why should you listen so attentively and carefully? Let's take you on a little trip back in time.

Think of the last time you became aware that you were truly being heard and seen because someone was giving you their full attention. Do you remember how it felt? Did you feel that you mattered? What happened as a result of it? Everyone is born with the fundamental need to be appreciated, valued, seen and heard.

Yet, in a fast-paced world of constant busy-ness and online access to the world through technology, many parents no longer take the time to listen to their children, some partners barely engage with each other while eating out, each respectively focussed on their phone, face-to-face communication in businesses is reduced, friends gathered together are constantly checking their social media feed or exchanging quick messages etc. How often do you have conversations when someone is truly listening to you, your struggles and your dreams?

In establishing the reason behind the importance of listening, we have come back to emotion, to the feeling of connection that is born from active listening and to how it makes someone feel to be heard and seen. Emotion wins over logic, and people buy on emotion.

What is active listening? It is, as I have discovered, on being told that I listened differently to others, a rare skill in today's world, in spite of being the secret to connection. Most people will half listen to what you say, taking in distractedly what you are talking about, hearing only some of the words and only getting the gist. This is passive listening.

A skilled sales specialist will listen to all the words; they will reflect back on what they hear, paraphrase, summarise, and encourage the client to develop their thinking. They will also hear the unspoken words, the silence, because silence speaks volumes. They will not judge or offer their own opinions. They will remain neutral, all the while showing genuine interest and understanding, asking for clarification where required. To overcome objections is to fully understand what the person is objecting to and the why behind the why, not just the first-level why, so gathering as much information as possible makes all the difference.

Ethical selling is only possible through empathetic, inquisitive, considered listening because your responsibility to the buyer is to ensure that you have collected enough information about the specifics of their situation, about their challenges and desires to be confident that the product being sold has the potential to deliver the ideal outcome. So, remember – detach yourself from your desired outcome, temporarily forgetting what you want, to focus on what the other party truly needs. Make them feel heard and important. Listen to the silence. Dig deep. Help them connect to their feelings. Then, reap the rewards that come from patiently prioritising them.

I would love to tell you that becoming a natural at selling is all about technique and understanding of the above principles, but my own foray into the world of sales taught me that mastering those was only the first step into a journey often rendered bumpy and challenging by a number of outdated, limiting beliefs.

Money blocks, feeling that you do not deserve to receive what you want, having been taught that it is wrong to ask what you want (especially money), wrong to ask for money in exchange for your help, having had your voice quietened too many times as a child, having been dismissed, ignored, ridiculed are all common issues that will need resolving for anyone wishing to master the art of selling kindly and successfully.

Acknowledging one's own worth and unique selling point is also crucial. There is no one else like you out there; you are the only person with your experience and expertise, and that means that you bring to the world something uniquely valuable, a unique perspective and a unique set of skills. It is easy to dismiss what we do so effortlessly. Yet, the very thing which we do naturally and easily but which others struggle to do is our USP.

Do not sell yourself short. There are many people out there who need exactly what you have to offer, but I have come to realise that very few people see what is truly special about themselves, which is precisely why I have made it my mission to use my gift to see people's unique magic and style to coach as many people as possible to clear the old debris standing in the way of seeing their own worth so they can live a truly uncompromised life.

'You can have it all'– five words which changed my life as I heard them spoken by Marisa Peer, founder of Rapid Transformation Therapy and world-renowned speaker, in March 2020. Until then, I had lived with the deeply ingrained parental belief that you could most definitely not have it all, that you had to opt for settling.

So, my message is the following:

Dare to believe that you can have it all. See your own worth, find your style and your voice and learn to sell your ideas and your expertise from the heart in a way that feels good to you because the world needs you. Selling will open the doors to having it all, to loving and living without compromise. If you do not yet have it all, keep going.

This chapter reflects my personal sales journey and my learnings along the way, but I hope that it will be helpful to you whilst also acting as a tribute from a challenging mentee with a neurodivergent view of the world to my amazing mentor and friend, Nick Staab, who I would like to thank for his unparalleled patience with my endless questions and need to understand why, for standing by me, believing in me and guiding me while I learnt that selling is not only serving but also loving and living limitlessly in more ways than one.

This would not be complete without extending my deep gratitude to Nick's unquestionably Elite Sales Academy, a truly inspiring, supportive, heart-led and visionary community to the image of its leader and founder. Journeying with all of you has been invaluable.

My Top Tips:

Tip 1: Make it all about the other person. Hone the art of active, inquisitive listening – truly absorb both their spoken and unspoken words. Dive deep into their thoughts and emotions, demonstrating authentic empathy and profound understanding.

Tip 2: Find what you love, love what you do, and sell from a place of love for all those you love, especially yourself.

Tip 3: Dare to believe that you can and deserve to have it all. Sing your unique song with authentic style, ride the waves with total trust, dance around the objections with gliding grace, and limitless living is already yours.

CHAPTER 20

From Wellness Consultant to Empowering Elite Sales Specialist: My Journey of Transformation

JOAN BARR

'The biggest adventure you can take is to live the life of your dreams.'

- Oprah Winfrey

As a natural health and wellness consultant, my journey began with a deep passion for empowering others to take control of their physical and mental well-being. Little did I know that this path would lead me to a profound transformation, unveiling the power of sales and the art of serving others. In this captivating story, I will share the remarkable journey that shaped me into an Elite Sales Specialist, enabling me to make a positive impact on the lives of women who are going through hormonal changes.

A Leap of Faith

My journey commenced in October 2003 when I courageously left behind my life as a school administrative secretary in Georgetown, Guyana, to join my father and his family in the United Kingdom. With an eager longing for the father-daughter bond that had been missing, I soon realised that my father's controlling nature would challenge our relationship. Determined to forge my own path, I made the difficult decision to remove myself from his premises, which unfortunately strained my relationships with my half-sister, half-brother, and stepmom. However, amidst these challenges, I resolved to focus on personal growth, enrolling in health courses through Newbury College and the Open University, which opened doors to opportunities within the health sector.

A Foundation of Care, driven by my thirst for knowledge, I secured employment at a senior citizen care home, the Royal Berkshire Hospital, and my local GP surgery. Working alongside a vibrant medical team, I became an integral part of a busy respiratory ward, caring for patients with chronic respiratory problems. Additionally, I took on the role of falls champion, conducting monthly audits and ensuring the safety of our patients. As a member of the diabetic team, I managed and supported patients and medical professionals, contributing to their holistic care and hitting our regular targets. These experiences laid the groundwork for my future endeavours, shaping my understanding of the importance of empathy and compassion in healthcare.

A Shift in Circumstances

In March 2022, personal and family circumstances forced me to leave my job as a senior healthcare assistant and embark on a new path of working from home after being introduced to natural plant-based supplements that saved my mother's life and regulated my hormonal changes, I was determined to make a positive impact on women's health and wellbeing. I embraced my role as a part-time beauty consultant and health coach. Recognising that true beauty starts from within, I adopted a holistic approach to health and wellness. However, I soon realised that to reach a wider audience, I needed to enhance my marketing and social media skills.

The Discovery of Elite Sales

Driven by my desire for growth, I embarked on a quest to improve my skills and stumbled upon a life-changing opportunity - the 'Big Business Events' social media training program. It was within this program of February 2022 that I encountered an extraordinary speaker named Nick Staab, whose captivating message on sales as a form of service resonated deeply with me. Inspired by his sincerity, I eagerly enrolled in Nick's 3-day Elite Sales Bootcamp Program in May 2022 and subsequently joined his partnership academy program for the next twelve months, during which my confidence was transformed, and I am now equipped with lifelong sales skills that have helped me to apply effectively when handling sales challenges, such as customer objections, understanding the various personality types and adapting accordingly.

Empowering Women

Armed with newfound knowledge and having a burning desire to make a difference in the lives of other women who are going through hormonal changes, I was able to launch my coaching business, 'All Things Menopause', within the first month of joining Nick's partnership academy program. As an Elite Sales Specialist and Empowerment Coach, I now guide women in managing their hormonal changes and helping them to live their best lives. Through one-on-one consultations, speaking engagements, and workshops, I have the privilege of witnessing the transformative power of sales and services in empowering women to embrace their worth and navigate life's challenges.

Nick's mentorship and the unwavering support of his team have been instrumental in my personal and career growth by boosting my confidence, self-esteem, self-belief, and self-worth. Additionally, practise clear and persuasive communication to articulate my offerings convincingly all of which have played an integral part in my coaching. Strong communication skills will enable you to build rapport, address objections, and ultimately close more sales.

Reflecting on the Journey

Looking back on the past two years, I am astounded by the profound transformation I have undergone. From standing at a crossroads, contemplating leaving my secure 9-to-5 job at the local doctor's surgery, to making a profound impact on women's lives in the United Kingdom and beyond is amazing. The journey has exceeded my wildest dreams.

The realisation of sales as a means of serving others and witnessing the positive impact and transformational changes in the lives of others has ignited an unquenchable passion within me.

The future brims with excitement as I continue to empower and uplift other women on their health and wellness journeys, expanding my coaching program to serve corporate organisations, church groups and other social groups within my local community.

In addition, I was able to create my five-step coaching system, which is a framework for empowering my clients to understand their current mindset, challenges, strengths, motivations and how they affect their health and lifestyle choices. The assessment tools helped me to understand the client's personality, values, interests, and aspirations, as well as their areas of improvement and potential obstacles.

The Power of Sales from the point of service. Certainly, it refers to the ability to generate revenue and increase customer satisfaction by effectively selling products or services at the moment of interaction with our customers. It involves leveraging the customer's immediate needs, preferences, and emotions to maximise sales opportunities while simultaneously providing customer satisfaction.

Adapting a service mindset is one of the key lessons I have learned from my mentor, Nick Staab, that selling is serving.

Here are a few key aspects of the power of sales from the point of service:

Convenience: our customers often appreciate the convenience of purchasing products or services at the point of service. Whether it's a physical store or an online platform, offering a seamless and efficient sales process can lead to us having higher conversion rates. Personalisation by interacting directly with my customers has created the opportunity for me to understand their specific needs and allow me to tailor their recommendations accordingly. This personalised approach has significantly increased my chances of making sales with my coaching program.

Upselling and cross-selling: this point of service is an ideal time to upsell or cross-sell additional products or services based on our clients' needs. It has helped me to suggest relevant add-ons or upgrades based on my client's preferences, thereby increasing the average transaction value.

Building trust: rapport through face-to-face interactions or personalised online interactions has allowed me to build trust and rapport with my customers and my clients, which has also led to repeat business, trust, positive word-of-mouth, and long-term customer loyalty.

Having immediate feedback and problem resolution through sales from the point of service will enable immediate problem resolution. If a customer/client has any concerns or questions, they can be addressed promptly, ensuring customer/client satisfaction, and reducing the likelihood of returns or negative reviews.

Impulse buying: this point of service is often associated with women who are impulse buyers. By strategically placing enticing products or offering limited-time promotions, businesses can capitalise on customers' spontaneous purchasing decisions.

Overall, the power of sales from the point of service lies in the ability to create a positive customer experience, increase revenue, foster long-term customer relationships, and ultimately optimise sales strategies at this crucial touchpoint. In addressing these, it can allow businesses to drive growth and maintain a competitive edge.

In conclusion, my journey from a natural health and wellness consultant to an Elite Sales Specialist and Certified Professional Empowerment Coach has been a remarkable transformation. Through mentorship and unwavering dedication, I have discovered my true calling in serving others and making a positive impact on their lives and within communities. The power of sales and the ability to connect with people on a deeper level have opened doors

I never thought possible. As Maya Angelou wisely said, 'People will forget what you said, people will forget what you did, but people will never forget how you made them feel.'

It is with this sentiment in mind that I continue to empower and uplift others on their journey of self-discovery, helping them to recognise their worth and embrace the boldness required for their transformational journey.

Epilogue: A Call to Action

To those who still harbour doubts about sales, I implore you to remember that selling is serving. If you genuinely care about others and aspire to make a difference in the world you live in, I wholeheartedly recommend embarking on a transformative journey with Nick Staab's Elite Sales Academy Bootcamp and letting him work with you on becoming the next Elite Sales Specialist.

Remember, sales is not just about making transactions; it is about building meaningful connections and providing value to your customers. By embracing a service mindset, sharpening your communication skills, and staying adaptable to competitor strategies and emerging technologies, you can streamline your sales process. You will be well-equipped to excel in your sales journey, which will open lots of great opportunities along the way. By staying agile and continuously improving, you will position yourself for long-term success in sales.

With that said, I would like to thank Nick Staab and Dea Fileva for this wonderful opportunity to be a part of the Elite Sales Specialist anthology.

"Be the change you wish to see in this world." Gandhi.

Thank you,

My Top Tips:

Tip 1: Embrace a Service Mindset. Adopting a service mindset means prioritising the needs and interests of your customers above all else. Focus on building genuine relationships, understanding their challenges, and offering solutions that genuinely benefit them. By approaching sales with a genuine desire to help and serve others, you'll build trust and loyalty, leading to long-term success.

Tip 2: Develop Strong Communication Skills. Effective communication is essential in sales. Hone your ability to listen actively, ask thoughtful questions, and truly understand your customers' needs. Therefore, tailor your messaging to resonate with your target audience, highlighting the unique value and benefits of your product or services.

Tip 3: Continuously Learn and Adapt. The sales landscape is ever evolving, so it's crucial to stay updated and adapt to changing trends and customer preferences. Commit to ongoing learning and professional development. Attend seminars, workshops, or training programs that can enhance your sales skills and knowledge. Stay informed about industry trends.

CHAPTER 21

My Ongoing Fulfilment Journey

AISHA DOGONYARO

'Don't overthink it. Do it.'

- Aisha Dogonyaro

THOSE WORDS HAVE become my mantra. I used to wait for the perfect moment, crippled by the fear of making mistakes. Procrastination became my norm, leading to last-minute rushes. Eventually, I grasped a fundamental truth: there is no perfect time. I realised that my hesitations, though often successful, could have yielded better results with timely planning and swift action. Now, I understand the value of seizing the moment and not letting opportunities slip away. Each task, no matter how daunting, becomes manageable with proactive planning and immediate action.

My journey into sales was sparked by my fascination with properties. Over time, I have come to a profound realisation: sales is not merely about selling products or services. It is a profound act of service, a means of helping and serving others. This understanding has transformed my perspective, shaping my approach to sales as a genuine opportunity to make a difference in people's lives.

I recently took a bold leap into the world of properties. For years, I have harboured a deep fascination with owning and renovating properties, but I never took the plunge. Eventually, my interest in the property business intensified. There is something incredibly gratifying about witnessing the transformation of buildings, whether through renovations or the exciting process of a new building taking shape. The prospect of being actively involved in these changes has ignited a keen passion within me, driving me to explore and invest in the world of properties/real estate. I am interested in helping people, and I am concerned about housing issues, among other things.

I aspire to be a channel of blessings, lending a helping hand wherever I can. I understand the limitations — I can't solve every problem – but I'm determined to contribute in meaningful ways. Whether it is by providing shelter, promoting agriculture for food security, or supporting medical initiatives, I am eager to make a difference wherever possible.

Recognising our diverse skill sets and gifts, I believe in the power of collaboration. When we all contribute our unique talents, we create a powerful synergy. However, to achieve these goals, willingness alone isn't enough. We need resources: funding, connections, and honed skills. This realisation underscores the importance of mastering our sales skills, enabling us to acquire the necessary support. Using the power of determination, collaboration, and effective communication, I believe we can turn these aspirations into impactful realities.

My journey into sales began with my passion for properties. Initially, my perception of sales was tainted by the image of salespeople solely driven by meeting financial targets, often at the expense of ethics and genuine care for their customers. However, my perspective underwent a profound shift. I came to realise that sales, at its core, is more than a pursuit of profit. It is a noble act of service grounded in the principles of helping and serving others. This realisation has become the driving force behind my approach to sales, guiding me to prioritise ethics, empathy, and the well-being of the people I serve.

Years ago, I had worked in the marketing section of a bank for over seven years and utterly hated it. I then resigned and went on to pursue a postgraduate course. While studying, I started working for a government organisation. Though they served a purpose, doing all of these things gave me little fulfilment. I went on to further develop myself by doing another postgraduate course while still working. At the end of the course, I stayed at my job, still without any satisfaction.

Years went by, and I was stuck at a job with no room for growth or even promotion. I, however, found some sense of fulfilment when I was able to help people, either people from the public who were in need of our services or my colleagues, and solve issues even when they were beyond my official responsibilities. A lot of times, it involved me going way out of my way and taking things a lot more personally to be able to help especially when people were in dire need. When I was not able to fully help, even though I knew I had done my best, I still felt bad.

However, things changed with the onset of Covid-19, and I found that I did not miss going to the office. I also took the time to do some more studying and had a part-time stint trying to do some sales/customer service-related businesses. This did not last long, though, as I missed spending time with my family and decided to travel to spend time with them.

Some months later, I lost my dad and stayed even longer in Nigeria. I was glad, though, that I got to spend time with him and everyone else. I returned to work and, shortly after, lost my job, which, quite frankly, I was sick and tired of. Several things had been nudging me into properties, e.g., people reminding me of previous conversations where I had said I would get into the property business years ago. This was also a time when I was house-hunting and already disillusioned with having to rent and was looking to buy. I kept on meeting people – new people, old acquaintances, etc. and talk of properties kept coming up even without me bringing it up. So many things seemed to point to this, so I started attending property seminars again. I had attended a few in the past while I was still working but got badly burnt. However, this time, I decided to take another chance, and this has proven to be a much better journey than my previous experience.

In the course of attending these property seminars, I got an email invitation for a webinar, which I attended due to my hunger to learn more. It was while attending this webinar that I came to the realisation that, truly, selling is serving. This rang true for me while listening to Nick Staab, who was one of the speakers at the webinar. Nick was talking about sales with so much passion and genuineness and showing how we sell in one way or the other on a daily basis. Listening to him made me realise that selling is truly serving and is nothing like my bank marketing experience.

Though sales came into my life some years ago, I only took it seriously after this webinar and thus started on my sales journey sometime in 2022.

Prior to this, my only serious active involvement with selling was when I worked in marketing at a bank many years ago for over seven years, and I utterly hated it. I hated having to speak to people to open accounts with us or try to sell bank shares, for instance. Some of these people were not polite at all and acted as if the money was coming into my pocket, and they were doing a personal favour, which was clearly not the case at all.

Though there were targets to meet, there was no personal benefit for me, especially as I was not assessed the same as my colleagues, and I was unfairly treated. Though I did not know it initially, I eventually realised this was because of family background, as well as other forms of discrimination. This was a truly bad experience for me and has affected me even years later. Though some colleagues also felt exploited, many could not understand why I was so unfairly targeted.

The other experience I had with sales was during the Covid lockdown. I worked with an agency for one of their clients. This was a customer service/sales job. They had some after-sales care services, but it was more sales (ongoing sales, replacements, up-selling, etc).

It was nice to be able to serve people even without seeing them, but there were also some restrictions. Sometimes, you had elderly people who probably had issues with using the computer or sometimes just wanted to be able to talk with people; however, we had time restrictions on calls. You had to handle everything very quickly, still maintaining professionalism, and complete your notes while on the call. The trouble was that a lot of times, the customers did not want to wait to have these notes done, and the time between a call ending and a new one coming in was hardly sufficient.

This was worse when the customer had a number of things that needed to be addressed in that one call, thus requiring a longer time on the call. Assessments felt like you had overstayed even when you dealt with the issues. Up-selling was sometimes a bit difficult, but some customers were pleasant, and even when they did not want any extra from what they called for, they were still pleasant while others were not. It also felt a bit like it was just the numbers we were looking at; even though we were expected to have some "small talk", it still counted as part of the handling time.

While the job was flexible to a large extent, the payment was very low, and getting available hours was difficult, so you sometimes could not complete your expected weekly hours. In addition to this, several times there were breakdowns with the system (so one ended up needing to go to the technical support team (which resulted in no pay, as you were not attending to customers). I was initially excited about a new line of work but soon would start panicking when it was almost time to start work. That would happen for various reasons, like the fear of exceeding the average handling time on a call.

All these previous experiences and, of course, the old perception of the sleazy used car salesman did not leave a positive impression on me regarding sales. With all said about my previous experiences, it was a pleasant surprise when I came to learn that selling is serving and to realise further that we do use sales skills daily (if not all the time).

During my sales journey, I have learned from mentors, facilitators, and the like, but I have also met people who have been sources of encouragement to me. I have made new friends who, although different, are generally of like minds. Over time, some have become even closer, and we can discuss various things and help each other. It is like a community or a family. I feel like I am in a safe place and can ask questions and even ask for help, whether it is about registering a company or about creating a business website.

I have always enjoyed learning new things, and now, starting on my property journey, I have come to see the importance of sales in various aspects of life. Now, I see this come in whether it is directly linked to the business or in my daily life – getting my mother to eat a bit more, my nephew to appreciate that he can't get all the toys he likes in stores, working on my CV, a business proposal, or speaking with estate agents, and potential investors. I have also found that having sales skills makes us more conscious and appreciative of people and things around us and thus helps us deal better with people on a daily basis.

Though I am not perfect, I realise that this has been a journey, and I am a work in progress. I certainly am more confident and have a better mindset than I did at the start of this journey.

I would like to spend more time with my family and for them to have the best. I would also like to be a channel of blessings, helping people where needed and where possible.

Over the course of this new (and evolving) sales journey that I am embracing, I have learned a lot, and I am still learning. It is all a work in progress, and I am keen to learn and put into practice the things I am learning.

My biggest learning has to do with my mindset. In the past, I avoided talking to people about what I was doing generally, even regarding my job and business. I have now come to learn that to sell, have clients, or serve people, I need to let people know what I do and see how I can serve them.

Just like Nick says, imagine if you held the cure for cancer or any ground-breaking discovery, wouldn't you want the world to know? Also, as seen in the gospel, you cannot light a lamp and hide it under a bushel. When you have something valuable, you are compelled to share it; it is an inherent part of serving others. Your light has to shine, people need to see your good. Sharing is not just about generosity; it is about acknowledging our interconnectedness, our shared journey in this world, and the responsibility we have to uplift one another.

Not everyone is going to end up being a paying client (at least not immediately). However, that should not stop us from helping them or pointing them in the right direction where and when we know what that looks like.

Similarly, I also learned and found that people are more willing to open up and talk to you when they feel that you care. One way of showing this is when you actively listen to them. The 80/20 listening rule is useful and further buttresses this. When we listen and care, they know we are not looking at them as a number.

My big vision is to grow a successful international business in properties, among other things by serving and giving back to the community and helping where I can. I would also like to share knowledge and see people's lives transformed.

With my newly acquired sales skills, I hope to not only have new clients but also have repeat businesses and referrals from clients, thereby building my client base. This I hope to do by meeting and exceeding their requirements.

I am glad to be on this sales journey, and while I am aware that I am a work in progress and we are all at various stages of our journeys, I hope that this chapter, in some way, serves to encourage you.

My Top Tips:

Tip 1: You can't light a lamp and hide it under a bushel. When you have something truly valuable, you are compelled to share it. It is not always about monetary gain, although that might follow. It is about a deeper sense of purpose and a profound care for humanity and all living beings.

Tip 2: Embrace the art of learning: stay open, and don't hesitate to ask questions when you are uncertain or unaware. Putting this knowledge into action and/or practice whenever necessary and possible is key. Remember, nobody possesses all knowledge; cultivating a teachable spirit is a strength. Be willing to seek assistance and guidance whenever and wherever it is needed. In this openness to learning and seeking help, true growth and understanding can flourish.

Tip 3: Practice gratitude in small or big things. I have discovered that expressing gratitude puts me in a more positive frame of mind. With so much negativity around, consciously appreciating what we have can bring a profound sense of positivity. Consciously write down things you are thankful for daily, and over time, it will become easier to do so. Count your blessings, name them one by one, and you will be pleasantly surprised.

CHAPTER 22

Mastering Your Seasons of Transition

ANGELA WIAFE

'Mastery is a skill set developed over an extended period of time, with intense training, via consistency, stamina, strength and discipline. It's therefore important to give yourself enough time to develop the skill sets needed to walk the high level of mastery you envision.'

- Angela Wiafe.

MASTERY IS HOW I have evolved over the years and how I continue to evolve as an individual.

I had my first business during Junior Secondary school, buying and selling to supplement my pocket money. I used to study French as an extracurricular course at Alliance Francaise Institute. They always had these foreign sweets on the campus grounds, so on the days when I would go for classes, I would always purchase a whole variety of these sweets to sell at my Junior Secondary school the following day. It was the best feeling for a thirteen-year-old to find a need amongst her friends and provide a solution which served both parties involved.

A few years later, after relocating to the United Kingdom, I started several side hustles while working as a retail customer service advisor and department assistant within three different departments over seven years. I mastered different skill sets and became the *'go-to'* person in the company as their training coordinator. I loved what I did and the people I worked with. I served above and beyond my responsibilities, always giving a hundred per cent of me. So, I thought nothing could go awry. Boy, was I mistaken!

I decided to expand some of my businesses to Ghana, using my 8-week paid holiday. While absent, my senior management plotted to give away my position to another, so I had to rush back from holiday. This distraction resulted in my business expansion falling through since I lacked the guidance and mentorship of an experienced coach. That was the beginning of my fall into the rat race.

Losing the expansion and fighting for my dream job - which I ended up losing anyway, resulted in huge bank debt and low confidence. I eventually ended up being *'just over broke'* (J.O.B.), trying to survive in a new role within the same company.

Then I started having a family, and like any hardworking and responsible mother, I wanted to have it all – being able to work and still be present in raising my children. However, during the pregnancy with my second child, my line manager wanted to enforce some unfavourable working conditions on me. I declined due to my pregnancy and the fact that I had to be available to do school runs for my first child. He then told me that if I couldn't work those shifts, I should resign.

I was furious beyond words! Why should I resign after giving the best of my youth to the success of this company? At last, I had no option but to resign. Would you believe that about six to eight weeks after my resignation, that manager transferred to another company because *he* couldn't handle the stress and strains of the store? What the heck? So, did he make me resign only for him to seek greener pastures elsewhere? Many mixed emotions and thoughts run through my mind. I was infuriated and regretted spending my youth in vain, building someone else's dream.

However, it was futile to fight back since there was nothing I could do at that point. I then decided to dedicate the next ten years to building my family and raising my children. I had to put my dreams on the back burner and prioritise being present for my young family. That became my new *F.O.C.U.S.* (follow one course until successful).

Four years later, the coronavirus happened in 2020, and the whole world shut down. This placed a huge financial burden on my family. I had three young children then – 6, 4 and 2-year-olds (which in itself is challenging), with only one income stream. I felt stuck, and I became desperate. With the majority of the world losing faith and giving in to their fears, I knew I had to sit up and evaluate my life. I identified that over time, my faith system and skill set had dwindled down. There was a huge gap between my current skills at that time, the skills I needed for the destiny I envisioned, and the skills required for the career I now desired. Therefore, I decided first to realign my faith system - which was my bedrock, before pursuing any career.

I knew I needed to develop myself more in the areas where I lacked the knowledge or competence for effective impact in the career plan I had. As much as I desired to give value to others through my career, it was best to rediscover my own values and then align my career with them.

Having stayed at home to raise my family, I needed both hard skills (e.g., specific, or functional skills like technical/computing know-how), soft skills (like active listening), an understanding of job expectations, and industry knowledge - after all, the world had drastically changed with the pandemic and the economy had transitioned to operating online.

The disparity between the skills I had and what was needed in this 'new world' made it challenging for me to fill open positions. I didn't want to fall within the estimated 20-27% of the under-skilled UK workforce who were unable to keep up with the demand of the new digital progression. I needed a plan and approach which would give me a head start for strategic training and the possibility of being hired by a company to achieve its objectives.

My speciality from previous experiences was customer services, sales and facilitating training programs. Keeping that at the top of my mind, plus how drastically the world had changed overnight, I considered a skill set that would execute any business or career strategy, both current and future - service.

'Creativity is the enemy of boredom. Therefore, wherever you find yourself and no matter what you do, anytime, anyhow, and anywhere, design, write, create, PRODUCE, and network!'

- Angela Wiafe.

I am focused and determined to evolve with the changing times. Therefore, I develop and position myself for success by serving and selling. I have understood that ***success is not what you pursue but the value you pour into others.*** It's good to give value, and the best value you can give of yourself is to ***build the capacity to provide solutions that are useful and needed.*** That has always been my focus in mastery. You attract success by who you become more than what you do. **Your '*becoming*' (growth) is greater than your 'doing'**. Most people miss it because they think they become successful by the things they do. The '*doing*' is only useful when you have '*become*'. **Your evolution is more important than your doing**. The most important thing about success is not what you obtain but the version of you that must be attained to have that result. Through mastery, you become aware of mediocrity and, therefore, strive to be effective, disciplined, and well-cultured.

Thus, in my journey to mastery, I discovered a way to gather my thoughts, ideas, etc., and express myself through writing. My first published anthology was via a national poetry competition back in 2007, with the Young Writers Poetry Odyssey.

I enrolled in Elite Sales Academy at the time when my youngest was preparing for nursery. I thought to myself, 'Enough is enough; something has to change.' Enough with the struggle and self-pity and putting my dreams on the back burner. It was time to pursue my love for writing, training, facilitating and motivating others, and my dream of having multiple streams of income.

What catapulted this decision was the fact that I had had enough of being just-over-broke and the strains this was having on my family. I knew I had to do something to change this pattern. Sure, I was coming out of my comfort zone and stepping into the unknown and without any connections or networks. However, I had to do something different to manifest something new and different.

To quote Albert Einstein,

'Insanity is doing the same thing over and over again, expecting a different result'

and Jim Rohn,

'You are a product of the five people you hang around the most.'

Through mastery, I enhanced my personality by 'unlearning' certain limited beliefs, thought patterns, emotions, and actions. I 'relearned and replaced' them with new and better ones needed for who I envisioned myself to be. I broke free from the fixed mindset I had unconsciously learned over the years and transitioned into a growth mindset needed for who I desired and envisioned myself to be. For instance, as a stay-at-home mum, I had to start thinking like an entrepreneur and author. When I first became an Amazon number #1 international bestselling author in four countries and thirteen categories, I had to start thinking like a Marketer and Entrepreneur.

The real concept of 'sales' manifested in my transition from the crossroads of desperation, struggles and low confidence. As the saying goes, a *teacher will appear when the student is ready*. Such was my case – the Elite Sales Academy appeared when I was ready for a drastic change. I became a part of the academy's first founding members in a bid to better myself as an individual, add more value to who I was, and improve my serving techniques. Since my faith was an integral part of my life and an important factor in my decision-making, I aligned my journey in the academy with my business and purpose.

Having to master the skills of selling and serving was a daunting and fascinating journey. *I took responsibility for myself* and didn't blame others. I set specific, measurable, attainable, realistic/relevant, and timely goals. I took care of my physical, mental, and emotional health and improved my professional and creative skills daily by learning something new. I worked on my vision and spent my time, energy, and love wisely. I also invested in finding a business coach and mentor.

Through mastery and serving, I have learnt how to invest daily in strategic relationships like family and friends, how to set boundaries, when and how to reward myself, and how to differentiate between my goals and other people's goals. I have learned that if you change how, you look at things, the things you see change.

Paul Deitch said,

'Feedback is the breakfast of champions'.

I have learnt through the Elite Sales Academy (E.S.A.) that confidence (through knowledge, experience, and certainty) matters and its attractiveness is one of the key assets you need in any environment. Second to that is a community that supports your dreams! This drives me to commit to life-long learning and to implement that education through discipline and consistency. My confidence increases each time I take more action in mastery. This means that I spend less time doubting and second-guessing myself and more time expanding my capacity and improving myself.

Since becoming an E.S.A. student, I've invested in countless coaches for different things and have gone on to write a total of 14 international bestselling anthologies. I work as a writing coach, a facilitator, and an international course-room mentor at Xcellence Leadership University Institute, and I serve as the director of Global Affairs at Xcellence Inc.

I make sure to surround myself with people who fuel me with faith instead of fear. I have partnered and collaborated with several professional powerhouses in the industries in which I operate. I am privileged to motivate and speak at the unit training sessions of a group of network professionals and beauty consultants with the knowledge I have learnt from various masterminds.

Providing solutions and mastering serving have made me a better listener. I am intentional about the people I hang around with and those I allow to hang around me (i.e., your network is your net worth). I continue to master how to handle objections better to produce a win-win situation that is beneficial to both my clients and who I am. PRACTICE MAKES PROGRESS!

Using the *'give first'* model, I keep expanding my comfort zone by putting myself forward. My belief system is what drives me as a faith entrepreneur, so I find opportunities that support these personal values. I also write poetry for charitable projects (*The Giving Book: From Our Hearts To Yours*, volumes one and three), as well as offer to read my poetry to others (something I did during the first-ever E.S.A. boot camp back in February 2022). It was through this 'give first' model that I was invited to collaborate on charity projects and my first Amazon number one international bestselling book in four countries (back in September 2022) – *Modern Day Miracles Experienced by Ordinary People*.

I have greatly improved since then, with several international magazine features with a combined distribution of over 160 countries, since December 2022, being nominated as an ambassador for an international media house and a nominee for the top 100 inspirational women of 2022.

I remember my interviewer asking during my Academy enrolment process if I could afford it given my background, as she didn't want to put me in a tight and uncomfortable situation. I remember telling her how determined and tunnel visioned I was to succeed. Determination is a positive emotional feeling that involves persevering towards a difficult goal despite facing obstacles. I had such a strong resolve back then to break the mould because I was tired and tired of being tired.

I have come to understand that great things can and do happen in unexpected ways when you take that bold leap of faith to step outside your comfort zone. Miracles do happen, and growth takes place as you overcome the challenges that come your way. Since then, I have continued adding value to myself through leadership courses and then pouring value into others by going above and beyond in my service.

As a visionary, I know that proximity, networking and partnering with others, plus collaboration, ARE key. Also, I have harnessed the power of investing in coaches and mentors to position myself for global visibility - their expertise will cut down your learning journey from decades to days.

My motivational mantra is to make a global impact one person at a time.

My children inspire me to be better. My focus is to empower and equip them with the quality of life they need to become great legacies for their generation. My children are my legacy. Therefore, I work smartly in order to be present in their early years foundation. It is my strongest desire and vision to equip and empower them with the tools, skills, and knowledge so they can be deeply rooted in excellence for their generation. Secondly, as much as I love uniqueness, I also love diverse cultures. My desire, therefore, is to travel around the world for a more rounded inspiration and to give back to my community through humanitarian projects. I also understand my calling as a global leader, pattern breaker and trailblazer for my family.

My final inspiration is for the young people in my generation. I strongly believe in establishing a strong foundation in life so that young people are made aware that there are multiple options out there besides formal education. I remember when I started attending a variety of masterminds as part of my personal development journey, there were hardly any young people present. We are in an ever-changing society where the majority of the population are consumers instead of producers. This is why I have made it part of my humanitarian vision to advocate community-based leadership and to educate, empower and equip young people by spreading awareness and providing solutions.

Some of the biggest challenges I initially faced in my life and business were:

1. Finding creative ways to become resourceful in my projects. However, I am learning to overcome that through collaborating and leveraging strategic and advantageous partnerships with like-minded individuals and businesses.
2. Mastering the dynamics of my values, in placing God first, putting myself second (*because you can't pour from an empty cup*), my family third and business last. *Faith, discipline,*

consistency, and *determination* are the backbone of my life and success.

For as the body without the spirit is dead, so faith without the expression of actionable works is also dead. You must discipline yourself to take actions that reflect your idea of success and master them.

3. As a global visionary based in the UK, mastering the different time zones was initially a big challenge for me. As a mother with a young family, going to bed late due to international projects and waking up early due to family duties was strenuous. However, I had to discipline myself, reframe my mindset and consistently show up with my best self. Now, through practice and mastery, others marvel at my commitment and consistency.

Finally, my vision is to launch my philanthropic project officially – The Speak Up - Speak Out - Stand Up Initiative. Though it has been a gradual process, I am determined and focused to see it manifest on a bigger scale and provide solutions to many who need it.

My Top Tips:

Tip 1: Your mindset is the pilot of your life. Whatever your mind can conceive and believe, you can achieve (Napoleon Hill); whether you think you can or you think you can't, you're right (Henry Ford). However, it is what you learn *after* you think you know it all that counts! (John Wooden, legendary UCLA Basketball Coach).

Tip 2: You are your biggest asset. Invest in yourself and in a coach or mentor. Commit yourself to life-long learning and dedicate yourself to 'progress' and not the illusion of perfection. There's always room for improvement, with something bigger, better, and greater on the other side. Surround yourself with people who fuel you with faith instead of fear.

Tip 3: An elite specialist must be an innovative and creative solutionist, mastering the art of speaking 20% of the time and listening 80% of the time. Ask good quality questions - How do I reduce the chances of someone telling me 'No'? What is their problem? How am I going to solve it? How do I handle their objections? How are we going to win together? Engage your clients, be present, listen, and serve above and beyond to the best of your ability.

CHAPTER 23

Property Portfolio Accelerator to Create Halal Asset Legacy

EMRAN HAQUE

'A man lives up to the lifestyle of his close friends he mostly hangs around with. So, each one of you should consider whom he makes his friend.'

- Prophet Muhammad (PBUH)

I WAS BORN INTO a middle-class but noble Muslim family in Bangladesh, a typical developing country where the eldest sons carry a huge responsibility for their family. The parents expect that you, as the eldest son, will achieve the best possible degrees and get a higher-earning job to financially help your family, including your siblings. This constant pressure of achieving the best turned out to be a blessing in my life.

All my life, I have been a top student wherever I studied, from primary school to university level. I used to be loved by my teachers and my parents as I used to get top results whenever I would sit for any exam and get distinction and scholarships at every stage of my study.

Fast forward, while studying, I developed a love for teaching others. That's why, after completing my Master's in Economics and Econometrics at the Number One University in the country with outstanding results, I chose to become a lecturer at a university.

Fast forward, I came to the UK to do my PhD in economics at one of the top Russell Group Universities in the UK with a prestigious British Commonwealth scholarship in 1998. This gave me huge confidence and happiness in my life as very few university teachers from the whole country get such scholarships every year. This has made me financially capable while studying to help my family back home.

In 2001, as an exceptional case, I got a one-year lectureship contract at the university even before submitting my PhD thesis. Then, in 2002, I received an ESRC postdoctoral fellowship for a year, followed by another Research Fellowship in 2003 at another prestigious university for three years. In 2005, I joined my alma mater as a Permanent Lecturer, where I am now an Associate Professor.

My life was going excellently in terms of financial position and the mental satisfaction of being in the academic scholarly career I am passionate about. By now, I have become a successful author of many scientific research papers in top peer-reviewed journals in economics and chapters in different books, along with other successful economists.

At my social voluntary level, having noticed the deprivation level of the British-Bangladeshi Muslim community in the UK regarding education, employment, and financial freedom, I started working with my community to help them become the best of the Muslims and best of the citizens in the UK.

For this, I devoted my time during the evenings and weekends to visiting different cities, upon invitation, to give lectures and run workshops and group sessions to guide them to achieve the best in their lives.

Very quickly, I became known as a respected preacher and a Muslim Life Coach in my community. I developed thousands of followers who would love to listen to my talks and get my advice and counselling on their career and family lives. While doing this, I discovered my ability to fundraise for developing mosques and different voluntary community institutions!

As an economist with expert knowledge of Islamic Finance, I noticed that more than 80% of Muslims in the UK do not have their own property - they live in rented properties, council houses, or housing societies.

The irony is that for many Muslims, this was not due to lack of affordability, but rather, they couldn't go for conventional interest-bearing mortgages as it is not permissible according to their religious belief. To tackle this issue, I formed a company in 2007 where my friends and family members joined as shareholders. To grow our capital to a level to help each other buy their own houses, we invested in different projects in the education and property sectors.

However, in 2014, came the disaster for the initiative, and that automatically led to long-term suffering, social humiliation and mental torture for me! One of our projects lost the license, and we had to close that project, where we lost most of our capital. Even though all shareholders signed the project with a profit-loss sharing contract, and as a consequence, I was not legally responsible for bearing the losses of any shareholder, they started socially pressuring me (sometimes shouting, screaming, swearing) to get their money back.

The irony was that I never had any plan to make a profit for myself, nor was I taking any salary for the hundreds of hours I spent per month on the initiative.

Instead, I was considering this business initiative as my voluntary contribution to my community. Even after losing more than a hundred thousand pounds of my own investment, which was way higher than any other member's/shareholder's investment, I was the one who was made socially liable to pay everybody else's money.

As a result, my life felt untenable. I was socially (not legally) forced to start paying everybody their shareholding money to uphold my honour and dignity. As the company didn't have enough money to pay back what they were demanding, the company/initiative collapsed. Still, I had to continue paying them from my own pocket, using my hard-earned money from my academic job! I have fallen into an uncharted territory!

In my whole life, I have always been praised and honoured by my friends, family, and peers due to my talent, honesty, and sincerity. But now I am being chased and shamed by people for something I am not financially or legally responsible for!

I was literally paying the price for my honour!

The irony was that my closest friends were hurting me the most by betraying and socially harassing me more than anyone else! This led me to get into a deep depression. I started losing hope in my life. I would sleep for longer hours to forget the horror I was going through. I would forget about taking care of my wife and my children.

Due to this deeply deteriorated mental state, I lost the focus to carry out my ongoing world-class research on economics as I used to do! This has caused me to lose my co-authors, who were forced to wait longer for my input in our joint research projects.

The situation was so dire that between 2016 and 2020, many a time, I seriously contemplated that I would commit suicide had it been permissible in Islam.

At that darkest time of my life, one day, I came across a post on social media about the inspiring story of Colonel Sanders, the founder of the fast food chicken restaurant chain KFC, though I am not sure how true it was.

On the verge of committing suicide at the age of 65, he thought to try another time. He thought if he had anything he could do best, he realised that he could cook tasty fried chicken!

He went for this passion, and that gave him KFC. Inspired by this, I started thinking about what I am good at in addition to my academic career. I realised that I had never lost in any property investment. Whenever I took any property project for buy-to-let (BTL) or buy-refurbish-sell (BRS), I made a lot of profit for myself and my investors for the last 16 years!

On top of that, my credit rating has always been "excellent" (nearly 100%). So, I told myself that NOT everything is lost. Whatever expertise, experience, and network in the property market I developed over the last 15 years, NOBODY can take that away from me. This is my own CAPITAL, and I can utilise this.

Accordingly, I re-mortgaged my own property in 2020 from one of the Islamic Banks in the UK and bought two BTL properties. However, the net rental income from these two BTL properties was insufficient for me to repay the people for the price of my honour. I felt the need to earn more!

By now, I have learned that mere dignity, sincerity, and honesty cannot be the key if you want to serve your community. I started realising, with this harsh life experience, that I needed to make a lot of money if I really wanted to help my community successfully. For this, I need to develop independent businesses on my own, keeping my voluntary activities for the community completely separate from it. By then, I completely understood the meaning of a wise saying, 'Don't mix business with pleasure.'

Since 2020, I have been frantically looking for any halal and honest business opportunity where I can make money. I found many people offering online investment opportunities, but I couldn't trust any one of them as I lost my ability to trust people! I became too sceptical about anybody and everybody as being scams. Along with the property market, I looked at many different types of potential opportunities such as cryptocurrency, share market, foreign currency market, and so on. I couldn't feel confident in either of them.

Then, in the middle of 2022, I came across a few enthusiastic guys from Assets for Life offering training and mentoring services on Property buying services for investors. I found them genuine and honest in their approach, and I could believe what they were saying about their services. Still, with scepticism, I joined their bootcamps and was inspired to join their Partnership Mentoring Programs. One is "Property Deal Packaging", mentored by Jamie York and Dan Buchan, and the other is "Elite Sales Academy", mentored by Nick Staab.

By the end of the property deal packaging bootcamp of Jamie York, he asked what one thing you achieved from this three-day bootcamp. I said, 'The change in my mindset'. I have been helping my fellow friends, colleagues, and community members buy, rent, refurbish, renovate, and sell properties for the last 15 years, from which they made a lot of profit. But I never thought this to be a 'monetizable service'!

Being excited, I thought of forming a team of partners (several estate agents, builders, Islamic mortgage advisers, conveyancing solicitors, architect planners, and so on) whom I have been working with for the last 15 years and successfully helping each other without monetising, and together helping investors.

So, I formed a company called Ethical Assets Ltd, did all the compliances, and developed a team of partners to provide a whole range of property services, such as Islamic mortgage/re-mortgage, property sourcing, letting management, conveyancing, refurbishment and renovation, and so on. I not only introduce my partners to my investor clients for different services, but I stay along with them to provide my expert knowledge of the market as an economist, Shari'ah knowledge on halal asset building as an Islamic Economist, and the knowledge of my long experience in the property market so that they get the best out of all the services in my partnership network.

However, when I started trying to monetise my unique expertise, experience, and network within my community, I faced two new issues: 1) people were not taking me seriously rather they were surprised to see how I suddenly turned into being commercially focused from being benevolent for the last two decades or more, and 2) I was finding it difficult to sell the product and wondering what was missing in my sales pitch. Why are people not getting convinced with my service?

In the meantime, I found my answers when I joined the bootcamp and later the partnership mentoring program under Nick Staab.

Now I know that I need to transform myself from being a 'salesman' who begs his clients to buy his product/service to being an 'Elite Sales Specialist' who can choose which client he wants to serve. Then I realised I needed to place myself to my property clients as a 'Consultant' and gain authority over them. On top of that, Nick's Sales Specialist Script is phenomenal! After practising it and using it with tweaking for my unique property services, I have started getting the real interest of my clients. With his mentoring help, I have developed 'The Halal Legacy Blueprint', a 7-step system of helping busy (Muslim) investors who want a hands-free strategy to build a Legacy in halal property investing to leave their legacy for the next generation. With this system, my target is to attract lifetime clients who can rest assured that they are in safe hands in terms of guiding them for halal portfolio building where they don't need to waste their valuable time searching for every tradesman on their own at every stage of their property portfolio acceleration.

This amazing system has started working for me. I have already helped more than a dozen clients develop their long-term halal property strategy and another half a dozen clients in sourcing profitable property deals. This earning started helping me pay off the price of my honour. In addition, I am attracting many clients who want to take the whole range of services I am offering for their long-term portfolio building. At the time of writing this, I am at the final stage of conversation with an amazing investor, who is planning to sign a 'legacy contract' with me to re-mortgage his current properties and raise finance to buy a block of apartments (at least thirteen). My team will source all the properties and manage their letting and maintenance.

I am gradually gaining the confidence to say that at the moment, I, together with my team of partners, am the ONE and ONLY Specialist Property Consultant in the UK who can act as a one-stop shop to provide the whole range of halal property services including Islamic mortgages from all available high street Islamic Banks and Lending Institutions.

However, as I love my University academic career, I have no intention of leaving my job. As a result, generally, I have to utilise my time in the evenings and weekends for my property consultancy services, and I feel constrained in time to expand services to many potential investors. I need to hire someone to work for me as a Sales and Marketing Executive to reach a vast number of potential clients through social media marketing.

I thank Nick Staab! His amazing mentoring style has boosted my confidence to such a level that I am contemplating several other monetizable projects such as (a) 'Muslim Family Coaching', an annual counselling package for a family and their children, and (b) 'Productive and Positive Life Coach', another annual counselling package for those who are going through severe tests and trials in their lives. Moreover, I plan to write a few books on these subjects as I have compiled enough materials from the talks, advice, and counselling sessions I have been offering to my followers voluntarily for over two decades.

My most significant source of motivation stems from my unwavering commitment to helping millions of Muslims in the UK to become productive contributors to British society. As a first step, they need to be financially free, and what can be a better way of achieving it than by building a sustainable and growing halal asset portfolio for themselves?

Another added commitment I made to myself is to earn millions to spend for the poverty alleviation of millions back home in Bangladesh. To fulfil this dream, I need to work hard, build a solid team and deliver my specialist elite sales service on property portfolio to as many people as possible.

I am immensely grateful to Nick, my mentor, for this great opportunity to showcase my dream and my unique property portfolio system, 'The Legacy Blueprint', to inspire others facing similar challenges to take action and become 'Elite Sales Specialists' and fulfil their dreams.

One more thing I want to assert before I end this writing. I am gaining a similar mindset by hanging around with the great mentors of Assets for Life who have the millionaire mindset. I now believe that I can definitely do it!

My Top Tips:

Tip 1: Never mix your business with your pleasure. If you want to gain pleasure by helping someone, do not engage in any business activities with them. Keep your business away from them. Otherwise, you would neither gain profit nor gain pleasure.

Tip 2: The sales target should be a win-win for the one who is selling and the one who is buying. Never sell your product/service cheap. Then, as a salesman, your motivation would be low to serve your client, and your client would value your service less. As Jamie York says, "price you pay, value you get".

Tip 3: Surround yourself with the people you want to be like. If you surround yourself with optimistic (pessimistic) people, you will become optimistic (pessimistic). If you surround yourself with successful people, their behaviour and success will inspire you to take up challenges to succeed in your life. Surround yourself with knowledgeable people, then you will become knowledgeable.

CHAPTER 24

Mastering the Art of Selling as an Elite

HARRIET MWONGERA

'Selling is Serving.'

- Nick Staab

I COULDN'T AGREE MORE. In his book, 'Selling is Serving', Nick nailed it! Yes, Nick nailed it. What a profound statement! All this long, my approach to selling was on autopilot! It was just a 'job'. Get the product, then shift it to the customer, and while at it, bring back the payment for it. As simple as that. No strings attached. No relationship building with the customer. It was about, 'let's balance this out' as quickly as possible. There are commissions to be earned. The system was already planned and implemented; the structure was laid down on paper. It had to be followed. No time to waste. Get as many potentials as possible; let's do this! No wonder I ran out of the contact list! They all flew away like birds.

So, when I was rudely interrupted by a video clip pop up whilst I was busy scrolling down the YouTube channels in search of God knows what, little did I know that it was, in time, to be a blessing in disguise! It was the beginning of a serious mental de-cluttering journey! It was a journey to un-educate myself from the traditional practices and approach to selling that barely succeeded in closing any deals.

Without hesitation, I found myself already enrolled in a 3-day boot camp training, and nothing was strong enough to block my way to my 'salvation'. I needed to be taught and mentored by the real elite sales practitioners.

Selling has been stigmatised in the past and associated with salespeople who almost force their products and/or services to someone, regardless of whether it meets such people's needs. The main focus is to make a sale! In turn, a potential loyal customer ends up buying with little or not enough prior information about the product to suit their specific need at the time. This, as a result, leads to unsatisfied customers and, ultimately, the loss of repeat purchases.

However, an elite sales consultant knows the art of selling. They seek to build trusting relationships with potential customers first by adhering to the ethos that governs their professional conduct and as a true representative of the brand and/or business. This trusting relationship helps to ease up any tension and remove any prior negative perceptions about the product and/or service that a potential customer might have had and be willing to open up to be informed about the benefits of the product and/or service on offer, and how they can best be used to solve their problem.

An elite sales consultant would go beyond the urge to make a sale and get to understand the underlying issues, the issues that might have caused the problem that a potential customer is undergoing at the present time.

They help the potential customer to 'dig' deeper into themselves and re-discover the root cause of the problem. Then, they are more open and receptive to professional advice, as well as to be educated about what's on offer. And if they choose to buy what's on offer, it would be out of an informed decision they made for themselves.

An elite sales consultant is able to apply this masterly to a diverse set of potential buyers and scale in a volatile market of fierce competition. And the secret to this mastery lies in servitude! Yes, in serving customers. This is the Elite Sales Consultant's unique selling point.

An elite sales consultant's main focus is to provide as much as possible education and information about their products and/or services to their potential customer and to offer them quality service. As such, they differentiate themselves from the profit-driven sales personnel in the same industry.

The success and its sustainability are credited to the capabilities of an elite sales consultant who has decoded the art of selling. An elite sales consultant understands the magnitude of learning and keeping at it! Studying the current market trends through reasonable research and passing on such knowledge to potential customers in order to build a client base of well-informed and satisfied loyal customers. An Elite Sales Consultant always stays ahead of the game by embracing change and welcoming new ideas to resolve customers' problems. They also ensure that customer satisfaction is always the focal point of their service in order to foster sustainable business growth and profitability.

Selling is an art that ought to be learned. Otherwise, it wouldn't make any reasonable sense, as it were, to produce, may it be products or services, if the primary purpose was not to pass it on to the end user.

For there to be buyers, there have to be sellers! Sales drive business growth and its sustainability. Hence, there is more reason for businesses and emerging entrepreneurs to majorly advocate the sales function as one of the core drivers of profitability for the business and so invest in fostering training and development of sales talent across the entire business setting.

I believe that 'we' all are wired to sell. To sell to each other! Not necessarily for the sake of making a profit in monetary form, but a sale can occur even when an individual successfully manages to persuade another to buy into their perspective. I would refer to it as an inborn quality. Just ask yourself, who taught a toddler the art of lying in order to negotiate their way out of misconduct they might be involved in? Somehow, they would try to redeem themselves by trying to 'sell' their reasons for doing the things they know they are not allowed to do, even if they've got to tell a lie in order to escape the punishment or the telling off, by the responsible guardian to whom they are accountable. A toddler just made a sale! Whether the guardian bought into that lie or not is immaterial. By default, a sale was attempted.

Many times, we might notice that we sell our own ways to others by default, and just because there is no monetary exchange involved in such incidents, it doesn't make it less of a sale. Now, if the party concerned 'buys' into our ideas, by the conviction that they would benefit from such ideas, whether there is any physical exchange for the equivalent of the perceived value of the idea or not, a sale has occurred. There was a seller, the one who initiated the idea, and the buyer, who accepted the idea.

When I understood this fact, I reflected back on the journey of my life, from as far as my memory could take me, and realised that, indeed, it is true. We sell to each other regardless of the gains that come with it. A sale is a sale.

It might interest you to know that, actually, my first paid engagement was in sales after my graduation. Yes, I worked behind the counter, selling general hardware stuff, at an Indian's general hardware store. These included automobile spare parts and farming aids to local farmers alike. So, in essence, I could claim the title of a sales personnel/officer.

I can assure you that the approach to sales then was by way of ensuring to close a sale the quickest way possible by persuading the customer of how effective the item/farming aid was and explaining to them that they were getting value for their money, which by the way was true. The approach to selling was aimed at making the most sales, earning a decent wage and commission if one exceeded the set target for the period under consideration.

Fast forward to the millennials and Gen Z era, the game has changed! Customers want more than just the product and/or service on offer, pushed to them by sales reps, who have not much regard and appreciation of the power of relationship building.

They want to be listened to, hoping that someone could really help diagnose the underlying problems that are causing them pain and provide solutions to solve such problems. That is the reason why businesses and emerging entrepreneurs need to be more proactive in readiness for emerging innovative technologies, such as AI, to aid in diagnosing customers' problems and then offer the best solutions for their needs.

The 'traditional' model of approach won't suffice in the current ever-changing market environment, characterised by fast-changing trends and digitisation. Hence, there is a need for elite sales professionals who understand and respond to the dynamism of the market environment with solutions which are tailored to address the specific needs of the customer.

As an elite, problem-solving for the customers takes priority. Building trusting relationships and fostering a 'learner' approach is key to success as an elite sales consultant. Therefore, listening to customers' concerns and educating them about the products and/or services on offer and how they are the right fit to solve their problems becomes one of the profound fundamentals of building a sustainable business, guaranteed repeat purchase, as well as customer satisfaction and retention.

So, when I came across the Elite Sales Academy, and attended a 3-day boot camp training, it was a game changer for me. It changed my perspective about selling. According to the convener and course lead, Nick Staab, selling is serving! Wow! That got my attention as I was scrolling down YouTube videos. I said to myself, in almost an audible whisper, it is true! How come I never saw it this way before? I found myself asking endless questions, and my curiosity increased. I needed to hear more!

I reflected on all my past involvements in sales, both as paid and as a volunteer in different organisations. I was serving! Yes, I was serving all along. This encounter, with an intrusive video clip, that popped up to distract my attention whilst I was going about my business, has changed my life! I am glad I dared to listen through and register for a free webinar, which led to my enrolment for a 3-day elite sales boot camp training, out of my own volition.

I had to hear a bit more. Learn some more. I had to satisfy my curiosity. It was one of the best decisions I ever made. To gain professional skills as an elite. It was, indeed, my pivotal point. My confidence levels skyrocketed, and I became more self-aware and improved my communication skills, particularly my listening skills. I have now embraced the art of selling as a service to customers, which has helped me to shift my focus from the result-driven approach to helping customers to solve their problems. As a result of adopting this approach, we now have satisfied customers who are more than happy to pay the asking price.

The 3-day elite sales boot camp training exposed me to a better way to sell, applying the problem-solving approach model as an elite sales specialist. Unlike the old way of trying to chase potential customers and expecting them to buy a product or service, the new sales model puts the needs of a customer first. It is a customer-centred and problem-solving approach, more professional, and is based on building and improving customer relationships building trust, which in turn guarantees sales in a sustainable way as a result of serving customers well.

I fell victim to job redundancy after 10+ years of service. The news didn't come as easy. My income was lost. My well-crafted plans for a smooth lifestyle were abruptly disrupted. Even after almost a decade of its occurrence, the effect still lingers. It caused a deeply rooted emotional pain that no words can articulate.

The shock was too much to bear. It was a lonely journey to trend. I was overstretched by my financial obligations, worsened by the COVID-19 pandemic outbreak and the resultant lockdown that followed for three years. All these factors added to the emotional distress as it was almost impossible to re-enter the job market again.

So, I chose not to dwell 'there', in the place of pain, sorrow and pitying myself. I chose to rise up again, this time with an intention to reinvent myself again in order to remain relevant in the marketplace. I went back to university. I graduated. I won the battle of the mind.

Selling, from the premise of servitude, has helped to facilitate the healing process and to regain confidence, to rise up from the fall, and try again. Having had first-hand experience of the challenge of loss of income and barely making ends meet has given me an invaluable life lesson that all things come to pass! And at that moment in time, when such happens, we all have a choice to make. Remain in the fall or rise up from the fall.

I chose the latter. I chose to forge forward in life because my destiny beckons. It was then, and only then, that I was presented with the vehicle to bridge me to the path leading to my destiny, the purpose for my existence, to serve. That vehicle was *the elite sales academy.*

Now, I am on a mission to help as many people as possible who might find themselves in a similar situation and who would like to hope again. This is my contribution to humanity, to serve from a place of love and sell as an elite.

My Top Tips:

Tip 1: Brand quality. Get your branding right and let it sell your product and/or services. Good branding communicates to its consumers.

Tip 2: Identify your target audience. Identify your ideal customer group. This is important in that you are able to eliminate distractions and focus on serving customers.

Tip 3: Prepare your 'state' of mind. Your mindset is your valued asset as an elite sales consultant. Have an absolute belief in your product and/or service and that it is the best solution to the customer's problem.

CHAPTER 25

Sales Unleashed: Boosting Confidence to Seal the Deal

SONAL SHAH

'Success is liking yourself, liking what you do, and liking how you do it'.

\- Maya Angelou

THE ABOVE QUOTE resonates with me as it highlights the importance of self-confidence and self-acceptance in achieving success, which can be particularly relevant in sales, where being self-assured can make a significant difference in one's results.

I work full-time in corporate as a vice president in Banking, and when I started helping people in their careers and inspiring women to help them achieve their goals and elevate themselves to achieve more in their careers, I did a lot more speaking to inspire others and share my messages. After presenting many talks, organising events and activities and providing much support, I got recognised and won my first two awards in 2018. Since then, I have been featured in Forbes, became one of 'Brummell's Most Inspiring Women of 2023', and was named in Computer Weekly's Most Influential Women in 2022 and 2023, among many other awards.

I set up my business alongside working to monetise and help others through the services that I provided to help women gain promotions, be visible through good personal branding strategies and achieve their career goals. Then I realised there was so much more to trade and that 'sales' strengthens everything we do, whether in business or not! I used to think it was for estate agents or salespeople-related jobs. Contrary to the outdated stereotype of sales being a male-dominated area, I know we are seeing a powerful influx of women who bring a unique blend of empathy, intuition, and unwavering confidence to the table in selling.

I soon learned sales skills range from when you are at work convincing someone of the best action to take on a project, selling an idea to someone, influencing someone for a decision or ensuring the best possible outcome from coaching or speaking. This all involves selling the benefits of your service, and it underpins everything.

After this, I needed to know and be competent at sales to make sure my services in speaking, coaching and personal branding were kept on the shelf, so to speak. So, my passion for speaking is about how important diversity, equity and inclusion are for businesses or personal branding and the use of LinkedIn to secure a new role and better prospects and promotion in work. To know how to network effectively, help women in tech elevate themselves in their careers or even change jobs into technology, and in general help educate and advocate for more diversity in business – all of these were slow movers in my services for me, even though I had identified the problems. I knew the need was there for assistance.

I experienced a lot of frustration as I was not getting the leads or enough sales, I thought, 'Enough was enough, something has to change.'

I felt I was not cut out for sales and probably should stay in my corporate job and forget the additional income – on reflection, I realised this was a skill that I should not be without, and I needed to *do* something about this to help so many people and not do a dis-service in giving up as people required my services out there. After coming so far in joining the business circle, I was not going to give up.

All these years, I had gotten by and done well. However, I now knew this skill could be honed with more training, structure, and some practice.

Therefore, and luckily, I joined an excellent business training group, so I started using some new training they gave and implemented it very slowly by learning.

Although some of this was alien to me and took more confidence than I thought, I took all the help I could by attending the weekly session with the business circle expert and practising with other colleagues in this same group or at any chance I got! This would be while at work in the day job; for example, if I wanted to make any changes or push new ideas, I found a new way to sell the benefits to colleagues or managers, which worked!

It was hard, although some of us do it without even realising it, and I found that given a good structure and understanding of the unique value that I bring to the table, together with learning through experts, it comes together. Understanding your knowledge and skills holds the power that impacts your clients' lives significantly, and through selling, when you believe in your value when you convey this to your clients during selling, it soon becomes second nature to you as I understand my audience and know their needs and my solutions for them.

Having confidence in sales as a woman was such a transformative experience. In my early days, after contacting many people for leads (and this was contacting cold, either by sending messages or calls) without any results, I became more resilient each week as I became more determined to secure business.

Historically, sales have often been associated with assertiveness, a trait traditionally linked to masculinity.

As the business world has evolved, so has our understanding of effective selling. I believe it is not just about closing deals; it is about building relationships and fostering trust. As women, we have an innate ability to connect emotionally and can reshape the narrative, so confidence in sales is not about overpowering but about understanding, empathising, and solving problems for people. By embracing our authentic selves we shatter the glass ceiling and know genuine connections are or can be the bedrock of successful sales relationships. People can sense when we are being authentic and true, and I found through my experience people appreciate your honesty, and that builds trust. So, through being authentic and confidently being able to navigate this new sales landscape, it felt like a breath of fresh air to still be myself, and I find that leveraging authenticity is a powerful tool in the art of selling.

During this, I also became better and more resilient. I learned this resilience from so many setbacks, rejections, and obstacles along my journey, as balancing a senior full-time job with business takes a lot. Cultivating that resilience gave me renewed confidence that I faced each day, with the certainty that I could overcome my challenges. Each time I had a conversation or sent out an email, rejection became water off a duck's back as I knew the next person or the next person, and the next was another 'potential opportunity' for me. I know now that every 'no' brings you closer to the next 'yes'. This courage inspired others, such as some of my friends and colleagues.

When speaking to people, I found that my use of and skill in empathy became a superpower in sales as I listened to women about their stories at work and some of the different challenges and struggles about not being heard. All of this, through my listening skills and emotional intelligence, became a powerful tool in building trust with clients and understanding their needs on a deeper level. The advantage of using empathy and building solid relationships (which, of course, is essential in sales) led to more accessible connections with clients on a personal level, with trust and long-term partnerships made. Also, the sales process became easier for me by really listening and placing their needs first, and I began to tailor my conversations with them appropriately.

Confidence in sales is not just a solo endeavour when you are learning; it thrives in collaboration and I enjoy being part of a community and network of support through my training, where we all share insights from our experiences and strategies for mutual growth. When we collaborate, we bring out the best in each other, and that collective confidence propels the whole team in our group or network to success.

As I understood the client's needs and pain points well, this ensured better solutions, satisfied customers, and brought my unique perspectives.

***

I use selling as a way of life for clients to achieve their career goals and not sit in their comfort zone and increase their pay, sometimes even double it. This is all so useful and shows success by knowing that I sell to serve genuinely, helping all clients I work with.

After a time, once I started securing coaching with clients, I was confident in my approach to selling when speaking to clients. Self-confidence in sales is contagious, and confidence is infectious.

As I discovered, the more I displayed it, the more it inspired and created positive results, boosting my morale and client satisfaction - with even more significant effects from my work!

It was like a positive feedback loop – positive energy generated by a confident woman (myself) even got noticed at work. I was asked how I remained so positive and bold to take on extra work and be seen at work. So, success builds on top of success, and I found you gain more energy helping me navigate the business and day job. When people see that you are confident in the service or presentation or whatever it may be that you are providing, then potential clients are more inclined to believe in the value you offer.

I had taken additional mentoring, which also helped me confidently navigate the sales experience. I also made sure to document my progress and started with attainable targets for myself and saw how often I broke them or not met them by putting in milestones to achieve along the way. So, this fuels self-assurance and made sure I maintained my motivation.

I was determined to lead by example, and as a female, I wanted to break through glass ceilings and help others do this, too. I ensured there were no barriers to success and developed a powerful mindset.

This helped in educating others as well, and confidence is a skill that is not just an inherent trait; it's a skill that can be developed and nurtured. Women can build their confidence in sales through training, practice, and a supportive work environment, so find your group and make sure support is in place for you. In sales, where charisma and persuasion go hand in hand, we women have emerged as a force to be reckoned with, and I can see that we all can rewrite the script of success with finesse and confidence.

I find females easily have an intuitive grasp of narrative and are able to share compelling stories that resonate with clients on a profound level, which helps. As Maya Angelou, the renowned poet and civil rights activist, once said, 'I've learned that people will forget what you said, people will forget what you did, but people will never forget how you made them feel.' As females, we understand the emotional imprint of a well-crafted story outlasts the details of any product or service.

My confidence was developed and nurtured through various means:

Training. I attended specific sales training programmes such as Nick Staab's bootcamp which gave me confidence through some exercises and techniques for overcoming self-doubt with a thorough structure and process to tailor and adapt from beginning to end, right from before you even speak to a client, whether on the phone or face to face as it is also about mindset.

Practice. Consistent practice and exposure to challenging situations in sales. Regardless of what happened, I would continue, which boosted my confidence.

Supportive Environment. A place that fosters a culture of support and encouragement can help you build and maintain confidence in sales. I kept this through Nick's network, plus other networks of support through business and friends.

Ultimately, having confidence in sales as a woman is not just about career success but also personal growth and empowerment. It was a chance to challenge myself, overcome obstacles, and achieve my potential.

I do this by keeping attuned to industry trends, honing more skills, and expanding my knowledge continually, as knowledge is the bedrock of confidence.

In an era where digital transformation is revolutionising sales methodologies, it is good to embrace innovation. Sheryl Sandberg, the COO of Facebook, emphasises the importance of embracing change: 'The only way to find your voice is to use it.' To be successful, it is also good to leverage technology, data analytics, and social media to amplify your voice, connecting with clients in ways that were once thought impossible and through remote helps with flexibility for your clients.

I also found mentorship from successful women in sales is invaluable. See below:

Guidance and support. Experienced women can provide advice on navigating the unique challenges women may face in sales, from gender bias to work-life balance.

Mentorship accelerates career growth by sharing insights, strategies, and lessons learned. It empowers women to reach their goals more efficiently. Learning from someone who has walked a similar path and thrived is motivating and helps you learn, grow, and improve in sales.

Inspiration. Seeing women who have succeeded in sales can inspire confidence in newer professionals like me. Knowing that someone has walked a similar path and thrived is motivating, and when you see people you admire, it is always good to be curious and learn more from them.

Intersectionality Matters. It is good to recognise that confidence in sales varies among women due to factors like race, ethnicity, sexual orientation, and more. Intersectional perspectives should be embraced to ensure a more inclusive and equitable environment. Embracing diversity will bring many perspectives and approaches to your sales success.

Confidence, empathy, mentorship, diversity, and advocacy are essential in this process. Confidence in sales isn't a static trait; it's a dynamic force that evolves with experience. Oprah Winfrey, media mogul and philanthropist, embodies the spirit of constant evolution, stating, 'I believe that one of life's greatest risks is never daring to risk.' Women in sales, inspired by this philosophy, embrace the power of the pivot—being unafraid to explore new approaches, pivot strategies, and redefine success.

Finally, having confidence in sales as a woman isn't just about selling products; it's about reshaping industries, inspiring others, and driving positive change in the business world. To drive positive difference in the business world – have confidence in yourself to thrive at sales; this is ensuring you provide 'sales as a service' in the best way.

***

I have recently appeared in Forbes and won many awards, including from Brummell Magazine's Most Inspiring Women 2023. Without knowing how to sell, achievements would not be received; how would people know about the excellent work I am doing?!

I intend to share my skills and incorporate them into my Speaking at conferences and events and for my client coaching. They will benefit from this even more by knowing how to secure their next moves.

My book was also published in 2023, so I do not want it to sit on bookshop shelves and on Amazon without any sales!

Bringing unique perspectives and strategies to the table can lead to more innovative approaches, expanding the potential for business success.

The awards and recognition mentioned at the beginning are all not achieved on their own. In other words, if you are not articulating your services well for all to know, you cannot be recognised. It does not stop here; lifelong learning on my journey is essential. Sales, like technology, is ever evolving, and to stay ahead of new tech, trends, and client requirements, we need to keep learning, so I embrace it.

***

Remember, confidence is not something you're born with; it is something you build through action and experience.

In the dynamic world of sales, where every pitch, negotiation, and relationship builds the scaffolding of success, as women, we can stand not only as participants but as architects of change. Remember, our confidence, authenticity, empathy, collaboration, resilience, and innovative spirit create a compelling narrative — a narrative that transcends boundaries and reshapes the very essence of success in the sales arena. We should carve our paths with determination and grace. The future of sales is a harmonious blend of diverse voices, echoing the unstoppable force of us being more empowered.

Make sure you go out there, believe in yourself, and watch yourself soar and excel in all you do!

My Top Tips:

Tip 1. Mentorship is invaluable. Learning from someone who has walked a similar path and thrived.

Tip 2. Embrace Rejection. Instead of dreading it, embrace rejection, as each rejection is a unique lesson, like a stepping stone to refinement. Embrace rejection as a stepping stone.

Tip 3. Have Supportive Connections. For women in sales or anyone new to sales, it is good to cultivate a robust support network. You can share experiences, provide encouragement, collaborate and learn to revolutionise your sales journey.

CHAPTER 26

Always Invest into Yourself and Never Give Up

KAY ANDREWS

'Everything happens for you, not to you. Everything happens at exactly the right moment, neither too soon nor too late. You don't have to like it....it's just easier if you do.'

– Byron Katie

I SPENT MY FORMATIVE years in a housing estate in Luton, Bedfordshire, during the 1970s and 1980s. As a single child raised by older parents, I often felt like an outsider. My parents were significantly older than my schoolmates' parents, and we lived in a flat while most of my peers lived in houses. This made me feel different, and I struggled to fit in.

My father was always busy with work, so my mother mostly raised me on her own. Despite what people who know me might say, I despised school. I simply kept my head down and persevered until I left at sixteen, with no desire to look back.

The first year I left school, I attended Barnfield College. I took several O' Levels to boost my qualifications, and in my second year, I successfully completed a computer course. After two placements, I secured a job at GEC Avionics in Dunstable. I worked in two shifts as an operator, responsible for maintaining the computer systems, including nightly data backups.

A year later, I moved to Telecom Gold, a British Telecom (BT) subsidiary in London, which ran an email service. I worked as a systems administrator, supporting the operators and maintaining the email, telex, and fax services. Eventually, Telecom Gold merged with BT.

Over the years, I had various roles at BT, working with helpdesks, supporting clients, and managing network services. I also collaborated closely with the finance team and senior management.

During this time, I became a parent to two wonderful children, Brad, now 26, and Emily, 24, as of the time of writing. To balance family life and work, I reduced my working hours to 25 hours per week, allowing me to share childcare responsibilities with my mother-in-law.

In August 2005, my father passed away, and I separated from my then-partner, Bill. I bought out his share of the house to minimise disruption to the children.

In July 2006, I faced redundancy for the first time. Thankfully, BT had a redeployment option known as the 'transition centre'. Employees were given the opportunity to retrain and move into a new role. I worked as a redeployment specialist, matching displaced employees like me to new roles. This was very challenging and introduced me to sales as I had to pitch employees to hiring managers with only a 50% skills match and also sell the roles to the employees.

In 2009, after a second redundancy spell in the transition centre, I found a position at Openreach, where I was involved in developing a new fibre order management platform. I collaborated with product managers in the UK to translate their requirements into a step-by-step process and worked with developers in India to build the software. I would tweak the process as required and gain sign-off all in a two-week window. My role required excellent sales skills to get everyone on board.

Over the next three years, I had various roles while my personal life evolved. I met my partner, Andy, and we moved into a larger house together in 2011. I oversaw the renovations and rented out my previous property. However, shortly after moving in together, Andy lost his job and eventually found a position in Bahrain. It took him away for four weeks every six weeks.

In December 2013, we had been celebrating Andy's 50th birthday with various meals out and weekends away in between his stints in Bahrain. He had been acting strange that particular weekend; the children were at their father's, and I was looking forward to spending a weekend with him. He lost his appetite and, on a Sunday evening, announced he was going out.

When he returned, I was watching TV in the lounge.

He came in, sat down on the other sofa, and then proceeded to tell me he had cheated on me for six months. My world turned upside down. I felt numb and in shock.

It was just two weeks before Christmas! This painful betrayal led to our separation, and I had to share the heart-breaking news with my children alone.

In the following weeks, I faced a series of challenges, from navigating the intricacies of the house sale to the startling revelation that I only owned 30% of it due to a clause negotiated by Andy.

It was a deeply unsettling discovery that left me feeling a mix of anger and self-blame. I couldn't help but question my own judgment and the trust I had placed in someone, not only with my future but also with the well-being of my children.

In the midst of this turmoil, I turned to my friend Sue for support. Her unwavering presence and understanding provided a lifeline during this difficult period. Despite the disappointment and frustration, I still considered myself fortunate to have escaped a situation with someone who no longer shared my values.

Fortunately, I had rented out my house, which provided a fallback option. However, this transition was not without its share of challenges. Little did I know, my tenant was struggling with alcoholism and had recently split from her fiancé. Leveraging my sales skills, I engaged in negotiations with the tenant to facilitate her move-out and collaborated with her parents, who took charge of addressing the damage done to the property in her absence.

Simultaneously, I managed the sale of the house, tackling most of the smaller items myself, meticulously packing them into boxes, all while juggling the needs of my two teenagers.

Despite these personal upheavals, my professional life was far from stable. My workplace was once again attempting to manage me out of the business, creating a high-stress environment. I faced a pressing deadline for performance paperwork due by the middle of the following week, on January 16, 2014. The deceit and lies that had recently marked my personal life left my mind in turmoil. Under the weight of enormous pressure, I battled anxiety and extreme stress while trying to fulfil my work obligations.

During this period, I made the decision to explore the possibility of purchasing another property while continuing to rent out my house. I had a plan to visit potential houses that weekend while my children were staying with their father.

On that fateful Saturday morning, as I was preparing to visit the new properties, I found myself in a rush. The staircase in my home had an unusual dog-legged configuration, and it was while descending the last set of stairs that I lost my footing and took a terrible fall. There wasn't a proper banister to hold onto, leaving me with nothing to grab onto for support.

As I tumbled down the staircase, my lower back struck one of the steps, and I continued sliding down until I reached the bottom, landing in the hallway. I remember sitting there in an awkward, twisted position, waiting for any signs of pain. At first, I thought I might be okay, as I could still wiggle my toes. However, when I attempted to move, I was met with excruciating pain.

Panicked and in pain, I realised the doors were locked, and I had just finalised the sale of the property. Calling an ambulance would likely result in them breaking down the door, a situation I wanted to avoid.

In my desperate moment, I reached out to my neighbour, Heather, who came to my rescue. She let herself into my home since I could not unlock the doors due to my condition. An ambulance was promptly summoned, and Heather accompanied me during the journey to the hospital.

I underwent an X-ray at the hospital, and the pain was so intense that I nearly passed out. Afterwards, I was wheeled out, and Heather's husband kindly came to pick us up. For the next two weeks, I had to sleep on the sofa, heavily reliant on potent anti-inflammatories and painkillers just to manage the pain. The hospital had only provided me with tablets and no specialised equipment. Thankfully, Heather was an incredible source of support during this challenging time, preparing meals for me and providing a wheelchair that I used to reach the downstairs bathroom with my son's assistance.

One of my dear friends, Carla, had experience working with stroke survivors, and she suggested that I reach out to the district nurse for assistance. Carla provided me with guidance on what to say, and to my relief, the district nurse arranged for the delivery of essential equipment, including a Zimmer frame. It was a tremendous help during a time when I couldn't move around or take care of myself.

The process of regaining mobility and independence was far from easy. I embarked on a gradual journey to practice walking again, focusing on building up my strength and coordination. However, it was a lengthy and challenging process, spanning several months and even now, I still experience pain. The road to recovery demanded persistence and resilience, but I made significant progress with the support of friends like Carla.

As the sale of my property continued, it became apparent that the process would take longer than expected due to issues within the property chain. By February 2014, another challenge emerged when my trusty old Meriva broke down. Unfortunately, the repair cost far outweighed its value, leaving me needing to find a replacement urgently.

I walked to the nearest garage and, after inspecting a couple of vehicles, I stumbled upon an old blue Mercedes coupe that caught my eye. The garage informed me that it would take a couple of days to prepare the car for me. In the interim, they generously offered me the use of one of their other cars.

However, what I didn't anticipate was that the blue Mercedes would need to be returned to the garage repeatedly over the course of several weeks for various repairs and adjustments. Each time, I engaged in negotiations with the garage to continue using their temporary vehicle while they worked on fixing my new car.

Unexpected twists and turns marked this period, but I navigated them with determination and adaptability.

Moving day, 17th May 2014, loomed, and my son was busy preparing for his GCSEs. I moved him into my house in the middle of April that year so he could revise and settle before his exams.

My parents had relocated to various places over the years. Finally, I settled in Shirebrook, some two hours from where I lived. It was in Shirebrook that my mother started to experience health issues. She had an upcoming appointment at the hospital scheduled for Friday, just one day before I was scheduled to move. I travelled up to Shirebrook on Thursday evening to accompany her to the hospital to ensure she made it to her appointment. Our journey began in the blue Mercedes, and everything seemed fine as we set off. However, as we were about two miles away from our destination, the car had broken down at a set of traffic lights next to a gun shop. We rang the AA, and while we waited to be rescued, I became concerned for my mother, who was not feeling well. We approached the owner of the gun shop, who was extremely kind and provided my mother with a chair to sit on.

Fortunately, a low loader arrived on the scene after about 45 minutes. The driver loaded our car onto the flatbed and listened to our predicament. In an act of generosity, he took us to the hospital, ensuring that we arrived just in time for my mother's appointment.

Following this, the driver transported the car to Halfords, where they could diagnose and address the issue. As it turned out, the alternator had stopped working, failing to charge the car's battery. Unfortunately, the needed part wouldn't be available at

Halfords until Saturday. This posed a significant problem since Saturday was the scheduled day of my move. What could I do?

In this moment of crisis, I reached out to one of my friends, Lizzie, who moved my children and coordinated with the movers I had hired to transport the large furniture into my old house. I couldn't have managed this challenging situation without Lizzie's invaluable assistance, and I'm immensely grateful for her support during this time.

I returned to work in July 2014 and joined a newly formed team tasked with improving order and fault management systems. My new manager, whom I'll refer to as Tom, held his first team meeting in the CEO's office. The atmosphere was tense as none of us were quite sure what to expect. In a rather assertive manner, Tom wasted no time in letting us know that he regularly played tennis with the CEO, establishing his perceived invulnerability within the organisation. Little did I know that this initial interaction with Tom would set the tone for what would come.

Throughout my time working under Tom's leadership, he consistently exerted pressure on the team to deliver results. He went so far as to devise an assessment across the entire Openreach organisation, within the Business Improvement (BI) discipline. This system added an additional layer of pressure and scrutiny to our work, setting the stage for what would be a challenging professional journey with Tom at the helm.

The assessment was initially intended to help employees identify gaps in their skill set as originally, we had all specialised in a particular BI skill. However, it later became mandatory, and failing it resulted in employees being unable to work in the Business Improvement discipline across the entire BT Group. The pressure led to many employees leaving, including high-performing individuals.

I had agreed with Tom to work four full days, providing me with longer weekends to care for my mother, who had been diagnosed with terminal cancer. I would travel to my mother's home in Shirebrook every Thursday evening and return on Sunday evening, ready for work on Monday. Tom, however, claimed I was not suited for the Business Improvement role and placed me on a performance plan, which devastated me. My mental health continued to suffer, and I didn't know which way to turn. I was in constant emotional turmoil.

My mother's health continued to decline, and I juggled her care with work responsibilities. I took two weeks' leave, and my children and I travelled up to see her in the hospital for Christmas 2014. Tragedy struck in the new year when my mother passed away on 6th January 2015. I informed Tom and took emergency leave to handle her affairs.

Upon my return to work, Tom wasted no time in pressing me to take the assessment. Although I managed to negotiate a brief delay, I was far from prepared or in the right mental state for the assessment. Tom, however, reassured me that I could retake it once I had identified my areas of weakness.

Regrettably, I did not perform well on the assessment, which was all the ammunition Tom needed to validate his belief that I didn't belong in the Business Improvement (BI) field. Consequently, he initiated the process of performance managing me out of the company. This pivotal moment took place in the

CEO's office at Openreach HQ, with Tom, myself, and Susan, my union representative, present. I was overwhelmed by the cumulative stress and challenges I had faced over the preceding years. At that moment, I felt a deep sense of despair and wished I didn't have to endure the pain any longer.

Fortunately, the intensity of the situation prompted an immediate halt to the meeting. This marked a turning point in my career, setting the stage for my eventual transition into a different role within the Chief Engineers team, where I served as a project manager for seven years before ultimately taking voluntary redundancy. Tom faced a similar fate, eventually being performance-managed out of the business.

Throughout these years, I discovered my resilience and determination. After leaving the corporate world, I pursued further education with the goal of starting my own business, allowing my children the freedom to avoid the control of others and pursue their dreams.

***

'Whether you think you can or think you can't – you're right.'

- Henry Ford

To provide for my family and empower my children to pursue their passions, I aim to give us all the freedom to define ourselves while advocating for the safety and well-being of others. My ultimate aspiration is to combat homelessness and eliminate it as a societal issue.

In pursuit of this goal, I took time to reflect on my life experiences and realised that every interaction, agreement, or negotiation hinges on the art of sales. To better comprehend this process and refine my skills, I made the decision to enrol in a comprehensive sales course. This step marks my commitment to gaining the expertise needed to effect positive change in our community and beyond.

'I believe in a concept that I've coined, "Selling is serving."'
- Nick Staab.

I had the privilege of meeting Nick Staab at a business networking event in Brentwood. During his presentation on sales, he emphasised how sales is intertwined with everything we do in both business and life. This resonated deeply with me, as it aligned perfectly with my own conclusions. Eager to enhance my sales skills, I attended a three-day event that offered all the necessary components to elevate my expertise. Subsequently, I enrolled in a year-long program, which includes weekly calls for practising sales skills with fellow participants and a structured process for conducting sales conversations effectively.

My Top Tips:

Tip 1: Set clear goals. Establish a destination or objective to aim for, providing a clear sense of direction from your current position to where you aspire to be.

Tip 2: Take consistent steps. Progress often comes from taking small, daily actions that propel you closer to your set destination. Consistency is key.

Tip 3: Embrace courage and determination. Approach your goals with unwavering determination and courage. Make it a non-negotiable commitment, especially when faced with challenges. This resilience will help you stay focused even in difficult times.

BECOME AN ELITE SALES SPECIALIST

Thank you for reading this far into the book. I can tell that you are an action-taker who found this book inspiring; otherwise, you wouldn't be reading this now.

Research states that out of every one thousand people who start a book, only thirty actually complete it.

As a gift for investing your time, money & energy into this book, I want to reward you with the next level.

I run a sales training community on one of the leading home study platforms called 'Skool'

I am inviting you to exclusively to join our Elite Sales Community.

Scan this QR code to join the exclusive Elite Sales Community:

Alternatively, head to the following link:

https://www.skool.com/the-elite-sales-community-4830

This community is all about providing you with the support and tools to help you on your sales journey!

In this community, you will have access to strategic advice, tools, and resources to help you as a newbie or existing business owner to accelerate your success. On top of that, as a community member, you will get exclusive invites to all of our top sales and business events lead by myself and industry experts. These events are great for networking with like-minded individuals, giving opportunity for collaboration and growth.

What is included:

- Free 'classroom' training materials.
- 'Community' posting of strategy insights and updates.
- Exclusive community access to webinars.
- Innovative training journey that includes our CPD-accredited training programs.
- Learn more about our mentorship training programmes.

I also run a three-day in-person training called the Elite Sales Bootcamp which is the sought after training where you will discover my seven-step Elite Sales System.

We only work with limited people on a monthly basis and getting a place on the training is application only, Access to the waiting list is only available to members of my Elite Sales Academy Skool group.

Find out more at:

http:// theelitesalesacademy.co.uk

https://www.facebook.com/NickStaabCoach

www.linkedin.com/in/nickstaabcoach

Instagram: nickstaabcoach

Printed in Great Britain
by Amazon

42240388R10185